WHAT *IS* SEX?

SHORT CIRCUITS
Mladen Dolar, Alenka Zupančič, and Slavoj Žižek, editors

WHAT *IS* SEX?

Alenka Zupančič

THE MIT PRESS   CAMBRIDGE, MASSACHUSETTS   LONDON, ENGLAND

© 2017 Massachusetts Institute of Technology

All rights reserved. No part of this book may be reproduced in any form by any electronic or mechanical means (including photocopying, recording, or information storage and retrieval) without permission in writing from the publisher.

This book was set in Joanna and Copperplate by the MIT Press. Printed and bound in the United States of America.

Library of Congress Cataloging-in-Publication Data is available.

ISBN: 978-0-262-53413-0

10 9 8 7 6 5 4

CONTENTS

A short circuit occurs when there is a faulty connection in the network—faulty, of course, from the standpoint of the network's smooth functioning. Is not the shock of short-circuiting, therefore, one of the best metaphors for a critical reading? Is not one of the most effective critical procedures to cross wires that do not usually touch: to take a major classic (text, author, notion) and read it in a short-circuiting way, through the lens of a "minor" author, text, or conceptual apparatus ("minor" should be understood here in Deleuze's sense: not "of lesser quality," but marginalized, disavowed by the hegemonic ideology, or dealing with a "lower," less dignified topic)? If the minor reference is well chosen, such a procedure can lead to insights which completely shatter and undermine our common perceptions. This is what Marx, among others, did with philosophy and religion (short-circuiting philosophical speculation through the lens of political economy, that is to say, economic speculation); this is what Freud and Nietzsche did with morality (short-circuiting the highest ethical notions through the lens of the unconscious libidinal economy). What such a reading achieves is not a simple "desublimation," a reduction of the higher intellectual content to its lower economic or libidinal cause; the aim of such an approach is, rather, the inherent decentering of the interpreted text, which brings to light its "unthought," its disavowed presuppositions and consequences.

And this is what "Short Circuits" wants to do, again and again. The underlying premise of the series is that Lacanian psychoanalysis is a privileged instrument of such an approach, whose purpose is to illuminate a standard text or ideological formation, making it readable in a totally new way—the long history of Lacanian interventions in philosophy, religion, the arts (from the visual arts to the cinema, music, and literature), ideology, and politics justifies this premise. This, then, is not a new series of books on psychoanalysis, but a series of "connections in the Freudian field"—of short Lacanian interventions in art, philosophy, theology, and ideology.

"Short Circuits" intends to revive a practice of reading which confronts a classic text, author, or notion with its own hidden presuppositions, and thus reveals its disavowed truth. The basic criterion for the texts that will be published is that they effectuate such a theoretical short circuit. After reading a book in this series, the reader should not simply have learned something new: the point is, rather, to make him or her aware of another—disturbing—side of something he or she knew all the time.

Slavoj Žižek

"For the moment, I am not fucking, I am talking to you. Well! I can have exactly the same satisfaction as if I were fucking." This is the example that Lacan comes up with to illustrate the claim that sublimation is satisfaction of the drive, without repression. We usually tend to think of sublimation in terms of a substitute satisfaction: instead of "fucking," I engage in talking (writing, painting, praying...)—this way I get another kind of satisfaction to replace the "missing" one. Sublimations are substitute satisfactions for a missing sexual satisfaction. The point that Lacanian psychoanalysis makes, however, is more paradoxical: the activity is different, yet the satisfaction is exactly the same. In other words, the point is not to explain the satisfaction in talking by referring to its "sexual origin." The point is that the satisfaction in talking is *itself* "sexual." And this is precisely what forces us to open the question of the very *nature* and status of sexuality in a radical way. Marx famously wrote that "human anatomy contains the key to the anatomy of the ape" (and not, perhaps, the other way around). In a similar way, we should insist that the satisfaction in talking contains a key to sexual satisfaction (and not the other way around), or simply a key to sexuality and its inherent contradictions. Hence the simple (and yet the most difficult) question that orients this book: What is sex? The way in which I propose to approach the question of sexuality is to consider it a properly *philosophical* problem of psychoanalysis—with everything that resonates with this term, starting with ontology, logic, and the theory of the subject.

Psychoanalysis (in its Freudo-Lacanian lineage) has been, among other things, a very powerful conceptual invention, with direct and significant resonances in philosophy. The encounter between philosophy and psychoanalysis has turned out to be one of the most productive construction sites in contemporary philosophy. It has produced some impressive new and original readings of classical philosophers and of classical philosophical concepts (such as subject, object, truth, representation, real), and opened a genuinely new vein in contemporary philosophy. At the moment when philosophy itself was just about ready to abandon some of its classical notions as belonging to its own metaphysical past, from which it was eager to escape, along came Lacan, and taught us an invaluable lesson: it is not these notions themselves that are problematic; what is problematic (in some ways of doing philosophy) is the disavowal or effacement of the inherent contradiction (or antagonism) they all imply, and are part of. That is why, by simply abandoning these notions, we are abandoning the battlefield, rather than winning any significant battles. In a similar, albeit not symmetrical, way, psychoanalysis (also in its clinical context) has gained a great deal by hanging onto and operating with philosophical concepts, and by playing a part in philosophical debates. For in this way it remained involved in the general intellectual landscape, its struggles and antagonisms, which it has itself brought to light, rather than enclosing itself in a safely circumscribed, specialized field of expertise and practice. And this was precisely the divide that Lacan kept pointing out, and which has been at the heart of his quarrel with (that is, his expulsion from) the International Psychoanalytic Association: the divide between psychoanalysis as a recognized therapeutic practice, appropriately confined to, or allocated, its field/feud, and what seemed to be Lacan's intellectual (and practical) extravagances which were, quite literally, all over the place (philosophy, science, literature...). It was here, and not simply in the battle between different psychoanalytic orientations, that Lacan situated the real divide. Apart from the famous short sessions, "intellectualization" was the key word and the key insult aimed at what he was doing in his "teaching" (which itself took place outside of psychoanalytic practice, and had a universal destination)—an insult aimed by analysts whom Lacan did not hesitate to insult back, calling them "orthopedists of the unconscious" and "guarantors of the bourgeois dream." The alleged "intellectualization" was not due simply to Lacan's persona (his own intelligence, erudition, ambition), but to what he recognized to be at the very core of Freud's discovery, causing its main scandal. "The unconscious thinks" is how Lacan liked to formulate the gist of that discovery. Ingenious dreams, slips of the tongue, jokes, as well as many (other) highly spiritual forms and creations, are all manifestations of the work of the unconscious. ... There is nothing simply irrational about the unconscious. Lacan also liked to point out how the biggest scandal provoked by the Freudian notion of sexuality (as related to the unconscious) was not its alleged dirtiness, but the fact "that it was so 'intellectual.' It was in this respect that it showed itself to be the worthy stooge of all those terrorists whose plots were going to ruin society" (Lacan 2006b, 435). In this precise sense, to say that the satisfaction in talking (or in any kind of intellectual activity) is "sexual" is not simply about abasement of intellectual activities, it is at least as much about elevating sexuality to a surprisingly intellectual activity....

There is thus little doubt about where Lacan situated the most important divide and struggle in psychoanalysis: "I would like to say, to those who are listening to me, how they could recognize bad psychoanalysts: by the word they use to depreciate all research on technique and theory that furthers the Freudian experience in its authentic dimension. That word is 'intellectualization'..." (Lacan 2006b, 435).

If, however, the encounter between psychoanalysis and philosophy has proved to be a most inspiring and fruitful construction site for both, it seems that avoiding this site has recently become more and more of the *mot d'ordre* (or fashion) in both fields. Philosophers have rediscovered pure philosophy, and particularly ontology; engaged as they are in producing new ontologies, they see little interest in what looks at best like a regional theory corresponding to a particular therapeutic practice. (Lacanian) psychoanalysts, on the other hand, are busy rediscovering the "experimental" (clinical) core of their concepts, which they sometimes like to present as their holy grail—the ultimate Real that they, and nobody else, are in touch with.

In this respect, this book goes—both methodologically and ideologically—against the grain of the "times we live in," refusing to abandon the construction site in favor of more polished "conceptual products," "services," or "singular experiences." The pages that follow grew out of a double conviction: first, that in psychoanalysis sex is above all a *concept* that formulates a persisting contradiction of reality. And, second, that this contradiction cannot be circumscribed or reduced to a secondary level (as a contradiction between already well-established entities/beings), but is—*as a contradiction*—involved in the very structuring of these entities, in their very being. In this precise sense, sex is of ontological relevance: not as an ultimate reality, but as an inherent twist, or stumbling block, of reality.

The question of "Lacan and philosophy" is thus taken up and tackled here at the point where the stakes appear to be highest. Sex is the question usually left out in even the most friendly philosophical appropriations of Lacan and his concepts; and ontology is something that Lacan saw as related to the discourse of the master, playing on the homonymy between *maître* (master) and *m'être* (from being, *être*). Ontology implies "being at someone's heel," "being at someone's beck and call" (Lacan 1999, 31).

And yet, or, more precisely: exactly *because* of this, it seems imperative to posit the question of "sex and ontology." It is here, I claim, that the destiny of the encounter between philosophy and psychoanalysis is being decided and played out.

As Louis Althusser argued in his powerful essay "On Marx and Freud," one of the things Marxism and psychoanalysis have in common is that they are situated *within the conflict* that they theorize; they are themselves part of the very reality that they recognize as conflictual and antagonistic. In such a case the criterion of scientific objectivity is not a supposed neutrality, which is nothing other than a dissimulation (and hence the perpetuation) of the given antagonism, or of the point of real exploitation. In any social conflict, a "neutral" position is always and necessarily the position of the ruling class: it seems "neutral" because it has achieved the status of the dominant ideology, which always strikes us as self-evident. The criterion of objectivity in such a case is thus not neutrality, but the capacity of theory to occupy a singular, specific point of view within the situation. In this sense, the objectivity is linked here to the very capacity of being "partial" or "partisan." As Althusser puts it: when dealing with a conflictual reality (which is the case for both Marxism and psychoanalysis) one cannot see everything from everywhere (*on ne peut pas tout voir de partout*); some positions dissimulate this conflict, and some reveal it. One can thus discover the essence of this conflictual reality only by occupying certain positions, and not others, in this very conflict (Althusser 1993, 229).

What this book aims to show and argue is that sex, or *the sexual*, is precisely such a "position," or point of view, in psychoanalysis. Not because of its ("dirty" or controversial) contents, but because of the singular form of contradiction that it forces us to see, to think, and to engage with.

Although this may not be evident from its length, this book is the result of many years of conceptual work. This work has not been linear, but consisted of going forward and then coming back to the most difficult issues from different angles and perspectives, and finally of cutting out a lot of things—that is to say, words. Inevitably, several parts of this book have already appeared, over those years, as presentations of what has been ongoing research. In order to avoid any misunderstanding in this respect, however, I want to emphasize not only that this is not a collection of essays (which is quite obvious), but also that the already published parts constitute material which, quite simply, cannot pass for being the same in this book. Not only because it was significantly reshaped and modified at crucial conceptual points and junctures, but also because it is only in the present work that it becomes what it is, namely, part of developing a central, book-length argument.

Recently, Lorenzo Chiesa's (*The Not-Two*) and Aaron Schuster's (*The Trouble with Pleasure*) books were published in this same series—books the topics of which intersect with mine in more than one respect. If these outstanding works do not play a significant part in my discussion, the reason is very simple: for many years we have been working on these topics in our "parallel universes," in friendly complicity, yet each pursuing his or her particular "obsession" and path into the topics. I thought it best to maintain the independence of our "parallel universes" here—a decision that should not be mistaken for a lack of acknowledgment of these significant works.

CHAPTER 1

IT'S GETTING STRANGE IN HERE ...

DID SOMEBODY SAY SEX?

In John Huston's movie *Freud: The Secret Passion* (1962), a very powerful scene depicts Freud presenting his theory of infantile sexuality to a large audience of educated men. His brief presentation is met with strong and loudly stated disapproval, interrupted by roaring after almost every sentence; several of the men leave the auditorium in protest, spitting on the floor next to Freud. At some point the chairman, trying to restore order, cries out: "Gentlemen, we are not in a political meeting!"

This is a very intriguing remark, pointing us straight in the right direction: that of a strange, surprising coincidence between politics and (the Freudian theory of) sexuality—and we will return to this coincidence in some of the chapters below. But let us first stop at the outrage provoked by the Freudian notion of sexuality (and especially of infantile sexuality). It is very easy, from today's point of view, to miss what is going on here, and to simply attribute this kind of violent reaction to the Victorian morals of Freud's time. Since then—we tend to think—we have learned to be very tolerant and to talk about sexuality quite openly; we know that "sexuality is nothing to be ashamed of," and that it is even good for our (mental and physical) health. We also think that Freud's discoveries about the determinant role of the "psychosexual" in our development have become largely integrated into the therapeutic practices of psychoanalytic lineage, albeit in somewhat diluted form. So it might come as a big surprise to learn that this is far from being the case. In 2009, Ofra Shalev and Hanoch Yerushalmi published a surprising study concerning the status of sexuality among contemporary therapists involved in psychoanalytic psychotherapy.[1] The results of this study prompted Kaveh Zamanian to publish an article in which he sums up some results of this study:

> With respect to the first theme, the therapists in the Shalev and Yerushalmi study tended to believe that sexuality serves as a defense against deeper and more difficult issues such as intimacy and self-identity. . . . In fact, sexual issues were viewed as an impediment to the goal of helping patients adjust to their surroundings and overall functioning. The third factor was a blurring of lines and utter confusion about intimacy versus sexuality. . . . They focused on sexual encounters rather than psychosexual aspects of development. Amazingly, two therapists expressed that "sexual issues should be treated by sexologists and not by psychotherapists." Notably, most of the therapists in the study did not separate sexuality from intimate relationships and even confused love and sexuality. As an example, one therapist concluded that his patients "rarely talk about sexual issues" and that their discussion of romantic relationships "never [has] sexual connotations." The fourth and final factor, and for me the most troubling, was the therapists' tendency to avoid sexual issues out of discomfort. Several therapists in the study experienced discussion of sexual matters as a "form of hostility directed at them" and even felt "abused by their patients." Again, shockingly, one therapist described one of her patients in the following manner: "It was as if he was thinking, this is therapy so I can talk about everything." (Zamanian 2011, 38)

Considering Freud's formulation of the *one and only* rule or imperative involved in psychoanalytic treatment, which is to say absolutely anything that comes to our mind, however unimportant or improper it may seem to us, this last line actually sounds like an excellent psychoanalytic joke. . . .

If this is the state of things in "psychoanalytic psychotherapy," we should not be surprised that the general *Stimmung* concerning sexuality, and particularly infantile sexuality, is not very different. This is in no way contradicted by the blatant media exposure and their abundant use of sexuality. There is no contradiction, because what is involved here is a systematic reduction of the notion of sexuality—its reduction to (different) "sexual practices" as constituting "sexual intercourse," and surrounded by obligatory sexual innuendo, that is, by a vast ocean of sexual *meanings*. This is clearly how sexuality comes across for the therapists involved in Shalev's and Yerushalmi's study: as naughty things that one does or does not do, and that one can eventually harass one's therapist with. If we understand it in this way, we can indeed agree with the claim that "sexuality serves as a defense against deeper and more difficult issues." The ironic point is, of course, that for Freud sexuality *was* the "deeper and more difficult issue" behind different sexual practices, innuendos and meanings—that it was something inherently problematic, disruptive, rather than constructive, of identities. Sexual activity appeared to Freud as redoubled by its own inherent impasse and difficulty, and as such it called for serious, ontological inquiry. What was, and still is, disturbing about the Freudian discussion of sexuality is not simply sexuality itself—this kind of resistance, indignant at psychoanalytic "obsession with dirty matters," was never the strongest one, and was soon marginalized by the progressive liberalism of morals. Much more disturbing was the thesis concerning the always problematic and (ontologically) uncertain character of sexuality itself. To the Victorians screaming "Sex is dirty," Freud did not answer something like "No, it is not dirty, it is only natural," but rather something like: "What is this 'sex' that you are talking about?"

Psychoanalysis does, of course, start out from the vicissitudes of human beings, on which it focuses its investigations. What keeps it from becoming a kind of "psychologized" human-interest philosophy, however, is precisely its discovery of and insistence on the sexual as a factor of radical disorientation, a factor that keeps bringing into question all our representations of the entity called "human being." This is why it would also be a big mistake to consider that, in Freudian theory, the sexual (in the sense of constitutively deviational partial drives) is the ultimate horizon of the animal called "human," a kind of anchor point of irreducible humanity in psychoanalytic theory; on the contrary, it is the *operator of the inhuman*, the operator of dehumanization.

And, incidentally, this is precisely what clears the ground for a possible theory of the subject (as developed by Lacan), in which the subject is something other than simply another name for an individual or a "person." Moreover, it is precisely the sexual as the operator of the inhuman that opens the perspective of the universal in psychoanalysis, which it is often accused of missing *because* of its insistence on the sexual (including sexual difference). What Freud calls the sexual is thus not that which makes us human in any received meaning of this term, it is rather that which makes us subjects, or perhaps more precisely, it is coextensive with the emergence of the subject. And this "inhuman" aspect of sexuality is what Lacan emphasizes in various different ways, including his famous invention of the "lamella."[2]

What is going on in the contemporary psychotherapeutic take on sexuality could thus be described as follows. In the first step, one diverges completely from the Freudian notion of sexuality, reducing it to a description of empirical features related to certain kinds of practice. Then, in a second step, one (dismissively) discovers that sexuality is exactly what one has reduced it to in the first step: namely, an overrated epiphenomenon. When one assumes, for example, that psychoanalysis claims that all our (neurotic) problems come from bad or insufficient sex, there is no more room left for—what? Psychoanalysis, precisely. This is the perhaps surprising point that Freud makes in his essay "Wild Psychoanalysis"; and it is exactly what the two seemingly opposite therapeutic perspectives (the one claiming that sex is the answer to everything, and the one dismissing sex as overrated) have in common: there is no room left for psychoanalysis in either of them. There is no room left for psychoanalysis, because psychoanalysis sees the impossibility of full sexual satisfaction—in the absence of all external obstacles—as a constitutive and integral *part* of unconscious sexuality as such.

The same goes for the idea that for psychoanalysis, (almost) everything has sexual meaning, and that to understand this meaning is the key to psychological recovery. To see how this misses the point, we simply need to bear in mind how Freud was led to his theory of the sexual as constitutively problematic. He was not led to it simply by discovering and deciphering the sexual meaning "behind" symptoms and different formations of the unconscious; rather, the opposite: he was led to it by stumbling against the "therapeutic failure" of the ultimate revelation of sexual meaning. Sexual meanings were revealed, connections leading to it established and reconstructed; yet the problem/symptom *persisted*.

And this opens the space for a different hypothesis: it is as if sexual meaning, so generously produced by the unconscious, were here to mask the reality of a more fundamental negativity at work in sexuality, to separate us from it by a screen that derives its efficacy from the fact that it is itself a means of satisfaction—satisfaction through meaning, satisfaction in the production of sexual meaning, and (as the obverse of this) in the production of meaning of the sexual. Paradoxical as this might sound, one of the primary tasks of psychoanalysis is to slowly but thoroughly deactivate the path of this satisfaction, to render it useless. To produce sex as absolutely and intrinsically meaningless, not as the ultimate horizon of all humanly produced meaning. That is to say: to restore sex in its dimension of the Real.

However, if we accept Zamanian's thesis that at stake in contemporary psychotherapeutic practices is a "defense" against something involved in the Freudian theory of sexuality, what exactly is this something? For one thing is sure: we must resist the temptation to take the defense against sexuality as self-explanatory; it is not "sex" that can explain that defense; rather, it is the defense that could shed some light on something inherently problematic about the nature of sexuality—something which repeatedly, and as if inevitably, puts us on the track of deeply metaphysical issues.

WHERE DO ADULTS COME FROM?

One explanation—let us call it the "progressive psychoanalytic explanation"—traces the discomfort in sexuality not so much to the difference as to the irreducible proximity or continuity between infantile and adult sexuality.

The paradoxical status of infantile sexuality as discovered by Freud could be summed up in two points. First, it exists, children are sexual beings; yet secondly, it exists in the absence of both biological and symbolic frameworks for its existence. It exists in the absence of both natural and cultural parameters. Biologically speaking, sexual organs are not up to their function; and symbolically speaking, children have no means of understanding properly and making sense of what is happening to them (sexually). One can under-stand that this kind of undefined, free-floating zone, unattached to any sym-bolic chain, can function as particularly sensitive—both in itself as well as in the imagination of adults. But there is a further and more important reason. If infantile sexuality constitutes such a dangerous and sensitive "zone," it is not simply because of its difference and contrast with adult sexuality but, rather, the opposite: because of their proximity. If infantile sexuality is something that is covered neither by biology nor by the symbolic ("culture"), the next and perhaps greatest scandal of Freudian theory consists in suggesting that, all in all, this state of things *doesn't change all that much* when we become adults. The "maturity" of sexual organs dramatically fails to make these organs func-tion as exclusive sites of sexuality, as well as to produce a solid basis for clearly understanding and making sense of our sexuality.

Jean Laplanche probably went the furthest to expose this conflict and dual-ity of the sexual by introducing the difference between drive sexuality (which he calls le *sexual*) and instinctual sexuality (le *sexuel*). In brief: le *sexual* is essen-tially related to different partial drives and their satisfaction; it is not innate, not object-based, and not procreative. It refers to autoerotic, polymorphous, perverse, non-gender-constricted, protean sexuality. Instinctual sexuality, on the other hand, is hormonally based, and more or less preprogrammed. This is the type of sexuality that arrives after prepuberty, that is, *after* drive or infantile sexuality. So that

When it comes to sexuality, man is subject to the greatest of paradoxes:
What is acquired through the drives precedes what is innate and instinctual,
in such a way that, at the time it emerges, instinctual sexuality, which is
adaptive, finds the seat already taken, as it were, by infantile drives, already
and always present in the unconscious. (Laplanche 2002, 49)

In the same line of reasoning, and based on Freud's "Three Essays on the Theory of Sexuality," one can sum these issues up by the following narra-tive: so-called "genital sexual organization" is far from being primordial. It involves a unification of the originally heterogeneous, dispersed, always-already *compound* sexual drive, composed of different partial drives, such as looking, touching, sucking, and so on. This unification has two major char-acteristics: First, it is always a somehow forced and artificial unification (it cannot be viewed simply as a natural teleological result of reproductive mat-uration). Secondly, it is never really fully achieved or accomplished, which is to say that it never transforms the sexual drive into an organic unity, with all its components ultimately serving one and the same purpose. "Normal," "healthy" human sexuality is thus a paradoxical, artificial naturalization of the originally denatured drives (denatured in the sense of departing from the "natural" aims of self-preservation and/or the logic of a pure need as unaffected by another supplementary satisfaction). One could even say that human sexuality is "sexual" (and not simply "reproductive") precisely insofar as the unification at stake, the tying of all the drives to one single purpose, never really works, but allows for different partial drives to continue their circular, self-perpetuating activity.

Yet there might be something slightly wrong with this narrative, at two points. First, in how it advances from the supposedly original, free, and chaotic multiplicity of the drives to an (always) forced sexual unification; and, secondly, in the way in which (much in line with Laplanche and his notion of "le sexual") it situates the properly (or "humanly") sexual of sexuality simply on the side of the drives and their satisfaction (as opposed to instinctual/reproductive sexuality). It is not that this is simply wrong; rather, things are slightly more complicated, and something crucial is missing in this account. This something concerns precisely the point of the encounter between the enjoyment involved in the drives (the surplus pleasure or the "other satisfaction" that tends to be produced in the process of the satisfaction of vital needs) and sexuality. It is precisely at this point that the strongest resistance to the notion of infantile sexuality is at work: What is it that makes, for example, the child's sucking of its thumb (or any other pleasure-seeking activity) sexual? Is it simply that we can deduce this retroactively from the adult sexuality in which these surplus satisfactions carried by the drives play an obvious and important role? This seems to be the answer of what I referred to above as the "progressive psychoanalytic explanation": if we look at adult sexuality, we can see that many of its elements (that is, many ways of finding satisfaction) are things that children "practice" as well, which clearly indicates the existence of some kind of continuity.

One major drawback of this linear account of sexuality and its development is that it leaves out completely the central concept of psychoanalysis, that is, the unconscious. Repression, it would seem, can enter this account only as repression performed on the sexual (content or activity), not as intrinsically and constitutively bound up with it. Hence the value of Laplanche's adjustment of this theory, which could be briefly put as follows: (Infantile) enjoyment is sexual because it is contaminated, from the very outset, by way of the child's universe being constantly intruded upon by "enigmatic signifiers," that is, by the unconscious and sexually charged messages of adults.[3] In other words, it is not pleasure or satisfaction as such, but the unconscious that makes a pleasure "sexual." The further crucial point is that these "messages" are not enigmatic only for children, but for the adults emitting them as well—this is perhaps the most fundamental example of the famous Hegelian dictum that the secrets of the Egyptians were secrets for the Egyptians themselves. What sexualizes the pleasure experienced by children is thus first and foremost the *encounter with the unconscious* of adults; not an encounter with an additional ("adult") surplus knowledge (incomprehensible to children and hence "enigmatic"), but with a *minus*, with something that first comes to them only as missing from its place in the Other. Infantile activities that seek pleasure for the sake of pleasure are "sexual" because of their entanglement with the *signifiers* which, by default, involve and support the unconscious of the Other. To repeat: what makes the enjoyment related to the drives *sexual* is its relation to the unconscious (in its very ontological negativity) and not, for example, its entanglement and contamination with sexuality in the narrower sense of the term (relating to sexual organs and sexual intercourse).

The unconscious thus enters our horizon as the unconscious of the Other; it does not start with the first thing *we* repress, it starts (for us) with repression *as the signifying form* pertaining to discursivity as such. (Further on in our argument we will relate this to the concept of a "minus one," which plays a crucial role in Lacan's later work.) The unconscious comes to us from the outside. This also constitutes a strong (Lacanian) reading of the Freudian (hypo) thesis of the *Urverdrängung*, primal repression as the ground and condition of all repression proper. In his conceptualizations of the unconscious and of repression, Freud was led to introduce the hypothesis according to which what we usually refer to as repression is actually and already an "after-pressure" (*Nachdrängen*). Actual repression or repression proper is already based on repression; repression is constitutively redoubled (Freud 2001a, 148, 180). Moreover, Freud emphasizes that it is a mistake to focus the discussion of repression solely on "the repulsion which operates from the direction of conscious upon what is to be repressed; quite as important is the attraction exercised by what is primally repressed upon everything with which it can establish a connection" (ibid., 148). Already in *Seminar XI* Lacan will radicalize this Freudian hypothesis by linking it directly to the signifying structure and to "a necessary fall of the first signifier" (Lacan 1987, 251). This "fall" coincides with the constitution of the subject: "the subject is constituted around the *Urverdrängung*." In other words, *Urverdrängung* is not a repression "performed" by the subject, but coincides with its emergence. And already here Lacan briefly introduces a theme that will become much more prominent in his later seminars, relating this instance to the Kantian notion of "negative quantities," pointing out that "minus one (-1) is not zero" (ibid., 252).

And it is in this perspective that we should understand one of the key emphases of this book: that something concerning sexuality is *constitutively* unconscious. That is to say: unconscious even when it first occurs, and not simply due to a subsequent repression. There is something about sexuality that appears only as repressed, something that registers in reality only in the form of repression (and not as something that first *is*, and is then repressed). And it is this something (and not some positive feature) that makes sexuality "sexual" in the strong meaning of the word. This is to say that the relation between the unconscious and sexuality is not that between some content and its container; *sexuality pertains to the very being-there of the unconscious, in its very ontological uncertainty.*

Before we examine this in more detail, we will briefly stop to consider another problematic notion related to sexuality: the much too simple opposition between the "subversive" chaotic multiplicity of the drives and "normative sexuality." It is beyond question that a lot of violence has always been done in the name of the alleged norm, but the question remains as to what is it that binds this norm to such violence: is it simply fear of the "untamed" multiplicity of the drives, or is it something else?

CHRISTIANITY AND POLYMORPHOUS PERVERSITY

According to the common perception, cultural (social, moral, religious) normativity promotes so-called natural sexuality (heterosexual intercourse) and tends to ban or repress drive sexuality, which is seen as perverse, asocial, serving no purpose outside itself, and hence escaping individual and social means of control.... But is this really so? Is it not possible that—beyond a very superficial level—this perception could be dramatically wrong? Christianity is usually taken as the magisterial example of the kind of attitude that bans drive sexuality and promotes only "purposeful" reproductive coupling. Yet it suffices to shift the perspective just a little bit (and at the right end), as Lacan does in the following passage, to get a very different picture:

> Christ, even when resurrected from the dead, is valued for his body, and his body is the means by which communion in his presence is incorporation— oral drive—with which Christ's wife, the Church as it is called, contents itself very well, having nothing to expect from copulation.
>
> In everything that followed from the effects of Christianity, particularly in πart... everything is exhibition of the body evoking *jouissance*—and you can lend credence to the testimony of someone who has just come back from an orgy of churches in Italy—but without copulation. If copulation isn't present, it's no accident. It's just as much out of place there as it is in human reality, to which it nevertheless provides sustenance with the fantasies by which that reality is constituted. (Lacan 1999, 113)

What is the point of this amazing passage, which rings so true? On the one hand, there is nothing necessarily asocial in partial drives: as autofocused as they may well be, they can nevertheless function as the glue of society, as the very *stuff of communion*. On the other hand, there seems to be something profoundly disruptive at stake in "copulation." For the kind of (social) bond it proposes, Christianity does not need copulation, which functions as the superfluous element, something on top of what would be (ideally) needed, and hence as disturbing. This is why even the "purest" sort of procreative sexual copulation is connected with sin. Or, as Saint Augustine has famously pointed out:[4] Sexuality is not the original sin (the latter refers to the original pair's disobedience when eating from the tree of knowledge), but the *punish-ment* for it, and the locus of its perpetuation—it is a subsequent addition to the original creation. In other words, in Saint Augustine's account, sexuality itself is problematic enough to be seen as a punishment, a curse.

Indeed, favored as it is in religion's doxa, "natural (procreative) inter-course" is utterly banned from the religious imaginary, whereas this same imaginary does not recede from, for example, images of canonized saints eat-ing the excrements of another person[5]—an action that is usually cataloged at the very peak of perversions. If we take a look at famous stories (and pic-tures) of Christian martyrdom, they are surprisingly full of partial objects in the strict Freudian meaning of the term: a real treasury of images of objects related to different partial drives. Saint Agatha's cut-off breast and Saint Lucy's gouged-out eyes are two of the most well-known images, portrayed hundreds of times by different artists.[6] Here are just two examples.

FIGURE 1.1
Saint Agatha by Lorenzo Lippi (1638/1644); Wikimedia Commons.

FIGURE 1.2
Saint Lucy by Domenico Beccafumi (1521); Wikimedia Commons.

Viewed from this perspective, Christianity can indeed appear to be centered around the "*jouissance* of the body."[7] Partial drives and the passion or satisfaction they procure are abundantly present in many aspects of Christianity, and constitute an important part of its *official* imaginary. In this precise sense, one could even go so far as to say that in its libidinal aspect the Christian religion massively relies on what belongs to the register of "infantile sexuality" (defined by Freud as polymorphous perversity), that is, to the satisfaction and bonds derived from partial objects, with the exclusion of sexual coupling. Pure enjoyment, "enjoyment for the sake of enjoyment," is not exactly what is banned here; what is banned, or repressed, is *its link to sexuality*.

In other words, it is clearly of paramount importance for the Christian religion not to acknowledge these polymorphously perverse satisfactions of the drives as sexual, while not banning them in themselves. But why exactly? Why this necessity not simply to fight all enjoyment, as is often erroneously believed, but to separate enjoyment from sexuality as neatly as possible; that is, to refuse to conceive of it in sexual terms? It is as if the strong social pressure put on "natural sexuality" (copulation) to function as the norm were there to hide an abyssal negativity of natural sexuality itself, much more than to keep the supposedly disruptive partial drives away.

In other words, this questioning brings us not so much to the cultural as to the "natural" aspect of sexuality. It is as if this "natural" aspect were in fact the most problematic, the most uncertain. There seems to be something in nature itself that is dramatically wrong at this point. The problem is not simply that nature is "always-already cultural," but rather that nature lacks something in order to be Nature (our Other) in the first place. Culture is not something that mediates, splits, denatures natural sexuality (as supposedly present in animals, for instance); it is being generated at the very locus where something in nature (as sexual nature) is lacking.

One way of putting this would be to say that there is no sexual instinct, that is, no knowledge ("law") inherent to sexuality which would be able to reliably guide it. Yet this claim can itself be understood in two ways. According to the usual perspective, this lack of sexual instinct (as a reliable auto-pilot) is perceived as something specifically human, induced by the human constitution (and the culture following from it). In this line of reasoning we usually say that while there is sexual instinct in Nature (in animals), there is none in human beings (who are thus the point of exception in respect to Nature). Humanity, at its most fundamental level, is thus seen as a deviation from Nature, and notably from the Animal. With humanity, something particular occurs that makes it decline from Nature, and complicates the way the laws of Nature function on the territory of the human. We will discuss this human/animal difference in more detail in chapter 4, so let us just briefly sketch out here what could be another possible perspective on this: to conceive humanity not as an exception to Nature, but as that point of Nature where its lack of "knowledge" (of sexual law) acquires a singular epistemic form. In this perspective, humanity is not an exception to Nature, a deviation from it, but the point of a specific articulation of Nature's own inherent negativity. There is knowledge in Nature ("knowledge in the real," as Lacan calls it), but this knowledge is lacking at the point of sexuation, and that includes sexuated animals.

What, then, would be the difference between the human animal and other (sexual) animals? A difference based not on human exception from nature, but on a different kind of articulation of a certain impasse of *sexuated nature* as such? Our answer will go in the following direction: human sexuality is the point at which the impossibility (ontological negativity) pertaining to the sexual relation appears as such, "registers" in reality as its part. It registers in the singular form discovered by Freud as that of the unconscious.

If we start out from a fundamental lack of knowledge (instinct) in nature at the point of sexuation (nature doesn't know how to be in the sexual sense, and we share this with other sexed animals), the difference is the difference between two *ways* of not knowing: a simple way, and a way that actually involves a singular kind of knowledge, namely, the unconscious. Animals do not know (that they do not know). Not completely in jest, we could say that sexuality is not problematic for animals because they do not know that it actually is problematic.[8] What distinguishes the human animal is that it knows (that it doesn't know). Yet at stake here is not simply that humans are aware, conscious of this lack of sexual knowledge in nature; rather, the right way of putting it would be to say that *they are "unconscious of it"* (which is not the same as saying that we are not conscious of it). The unconscious (in its very form) is the "positive" way in which the ontological negativity of a given reality registers in this reality itself, and it registers in a way which does not rely on the simple opposition between knowing and not knowing, between being or not being aware of something. And the reason is that what is at stake is precisely not "something" (some thing, some fact that we could be aware of or not) but a negativity that is itself perceptible only through its own negation. To be "unconscious of something" does not mean simply that one does not know it; rather, it implies a paradoxical redoublement, and is itself twofold or split: it involves *not knowing that we know* (... that we don't know). This is one of the best definitions of the unconscious (Žižek 2008, 457). As Lacan put it, unconscious knowledge is a knowledge that does not know itself.

The singular and revolutionary Freudian notion of the unconscious is thus not simply about not knowing as opposed to knowing. It is about a singular form of not-knowing as a form of knowing. There is a particular kind of knowledge that exists only in, and *as*, the very form of the unconscious, its work and its formations. And I am not talking about some kind of prereflective intuition—the latter may well exist, but it has nothing to do with the unconscious and its structure. The unconscious is the very form of existence of an ontological negativity pertaining to sexuality ("there is no sexual relation"). Because of its link to a singular mode/split of knowledge (I don't know that I know), this form is actually *epistemic*.

Let us now link this to our previous investigation: what can it tell us about the functioning of the norm (of purely reproductive coupling) in the Christian tradition? What exactly is being banned or veiled by this norm? It seems to concern precisely the *ontological negativity* of sexuation and sexuality as such. What one attempts to hide or repress in imposing the norm (of purely reproductive coupling) is not simply something else (for instance, a perverse debauchery, or pure self-perpetuating enjoyment), but rather the *something which is not there* (something missing). In other words: what is being banned is not the Signifier of the sexual (or its Image), but rather the (unconscious) knowledge of the nonexistence of such a Signifier. Sexuality is regulated in all kinds of ways not because of its debauchery, but insofar as it implies (and "transmits") the knowledge of this ontological negativity.

The quintessential biblical story that presents sexuality and knowledge as inseparably bound to the scene of original sin is thus pointing in the right direction. What exactly is it that Adam and Eve got to know when they ate from the tree of knowledge? In the Bible this is not clear at all. What is clear, however, is that the expression "good and evil" (*rov wa-ra*)—in the formulation "tree of the knowledge of good and evil"—does not refer to the knowing of, and distinguishing between, good and evil (this would already be a highly tendentious reading), but is actually a fixed expression denoting "everything" (as when we say "this and that"). Thus all the Bible tells us is that when they ate from the tree of knowledge, knowledge was imparted to Adam and Eve. And if we venture a Lacanian reading of this, we could add: not knowledge of this or that particular thing, but the (signifying) structure of knowledge as such. And what comes with the "(signifying) structure of knowledge as such" is the gap of the unconscious: the latter is precisely what distinguishes knowledge from information or data. In other words, what was transmitted to them was precisely the gap of the *Urverdrängung* as constitutive of knowledge. And this is why, once they ate from the tree of *knowledge*, the immediate result was an *affect*, namely that they found the sight of their naked bodies shameful. This shame is properly ontological: it appears at the place of the lacking signifier (-1), because of the signifying lack built into the structure of knowledge: it appears because no signifier appears there....

This significant link between knowledge and sex is not limited in the Bible only to the scene of original sin, but has a further and repetitive insistence. Hence the idiom "knowledge in the biblical sense." This particular way in which the Bible refers to sexual intercourse (as "knowing the other") is obviously not of the same kind as the other most common euphemisms for intercourse that we find there: "to enter," "to lie with," and "to go into." These are simply descriptive euphemisms. On the other hand, could we not recognize, in the way knowledge is used to refer to sexual intercourse, a signifying trace of the sexual relation falling into its own ontological void, which registers only as a peculiar (negative) epistemological score? That is to say: "knowing the other in the biblical sense" is to engage with the point in the Other where knowledge is lacking. And from the religious perspective, this lack of knowledge in the Other (missing signifier of the sexual relation) is no small matter. Hence the shame. The sight of naked bodies is not "shameful" because of these bodies as such, but because of what these naked bodies fail to convey, namely, the sexual relation.

We find a similar constellation if we consider sexuality on the level of the imaginary: all we can *see* in representations of sexuality is bodies enjoying parts of other bodies. In Lacan's words:

> As is emphasized admirably by the kind of Kantian that Sade was, one can only enjoy a part of the Other's body, for the simple reason that one has never seen a body completely wrap itself around the Other's body, to the point of surrounding and phagocytizing it. That is why we must confine ourselves to simply giving it a little squeeze, like that, taking a forearm or anything else—ouch! (Lacan 1999, 23)

The norm (normative prescriptions of sexuality) emerges precisely at the point of this lack in the representation. More precisely, the norm could be seen as *taking the place of the image* that "one has never seen," that of a body completely wrapping itself around the Other's body. This image, in its very impossibility, is its other side, it is the fantasmatic underpinning of the norm; it is what helps to sustain the norm, and our complicity in it. It is the fantasy sustained by the very imposition of the norm, and sustaining the norm in turn: the fantasy of the sexual relation.

The further crucial thing to point out at this juncture, however, is that non-relation is not simply an absence of relation, but is itself a real, even the Real. What does this mean? We must not make the mistake of conceiving the existence of the sexual relation as a fantasy, which psychoanalysis would invite us to get rid of, and to accept instead the reality of partial drives and fleeting pleasures ("squeezing" here and there) as the ultimate raw reality, as *all* there is. The sexual relation is not simply a fantasy of something that is not there, but which we would, for some reason, like to be there (why exactly we would be so eager for it to exist is not clear in this sort of argument). Why would something like the nonexistence of the sexual relation be "unbearable," if we can get actual satisfaction by "squeezing" here and there, by enjoying parts of the other's body (or our own, for that matter)? The lack of sexual relation is real in the sense that, as lack or negativity, it is built into *what is there*, determining its logic and structure in an important way.[9] This brings us back to the erroneous opposition between what seems to be a full positivity of the drives (in their very partial character) and the negativity at work in sexuality (as relational). What psychoanalysis teaches us is not that, because of this non-relation, we have access to only partial and fleeting pleasures and satisfactions ("squeezing" here and there). The claim is stronger: these partial pleasures and satisfactions are *already (in-)formed by the negativity implied by the non-relation*. They do not exist independently of it, so that we could have recourse to them, for lack of anything better. They are essentially and intrinsically constituted by "the lack of anything better": they are the way in which the lack of anything better (the lack of sexual substance or signifier) *exists in reality*. It is not—to put it simply—that we have, on the one hand, the pure positivity of the drives and their satisfactions and, on the other, this (catastrophic) idea that we need something else or more, namely, for them to form or represent a relation. And since this does not happen, we feel bad and erect the fantasy of the relation. The fantasy (and imperative) of the relation comes from (within) the very structuring of the drives. Let us now look more closely at what this could mean.

CHAPTER 2

... AND EVEN STRANGER OUT THERE

THE QUANDARY OF THE RELATION

Let us return to John Huston's movie Freud: The Secret Passion. The remark of
the chairman, trying to restore order in the passionate outrage provoked by
Freud's lecture on infantile sexuality ("Gentlemen, we are not in a political
meeting!"), does indeed point us in a most interesting direction, that of a
surprising coincidence between politics and the (Freudian) theory of sexuality. It is as if every time one reopens the question of sexuality, something is
decided that is of a political order. This certainly held true for the politics of
the psychoanalytic movement itself, and for the ruptures it produced within
the movement. But it might also be true in the more specific sense of politics as referring to what can be articulated around some fundamental social
antagonism(s).[1]

When speaking about psychoanalysis and politics today, one usually adopts
one of two attitudes. The first is to leave sexuality out, put it aside, and pursue other concepts, such as the (barred) Other, surplus-enjoyment, the
Lacanian theory of the four discourses, the Lacanian contribution to the ideology critique....All of these are of course crucial, yet they cannot be exempted
from the issue of the sexual without losing something central, namely, a conceptual articulation of a negativity at work at their core, sustaining them as
well as relating them to one another. There is also a second attitude which, in
tune with the prevailing (Western) ideology of our time, combines moral
liberalism (anything goes, and should be tolerated, as long as there is no
abuse involved) with political conservativism (of the status quo, in which
every zealous political engagement is by definition "pathological," unbefit-
ting to "normal," "non-neurotic" human beings). These two attitudes share a
symmetrical (albeit not identical) mistake. The philosophical and politically
more radical reading of Lacan dismisses sexuality as something that has only a
secondary, anecdotal, or "regional" relevance. And the liberal psychoanalytic

reading dismisses politics *as something* that is necessarily pathological (blind to the impossibility at work in it). The mistake of the first reading is not that it misunderstands the relevance of sexuality, but that it considers it *as something* (something which simply *is*, and can be deemed of lesser or greater importance). In the same way, the mistake of the second reading is not that it fails to see that an essentially different politics is nevertheless possible, but again that it takes politics *as something*, as a fully fledged entity with certain characteristics. In other words, it fails to see that politics is by definition the politics of the impossible (relation). What relates sexuality to politics is that they are not simple ontological categories but essentially imply, depend on, and deploy something which is not of the order of being, and which Lacan refers to as *the Real*. The Real is precisely not being, but its inherent impasse.

The Lacanian concept of the sexual is not one that provides the best description so far of a certain reality (called sexuality); what it does is develop a unique model of thinking a fundamental non-relationship as dictating the conditions of different kinds of ties (including social ties, or "discourses"). For this is what the Lacanian concept of sexuality is primarily about. It conceptualizes the way in which a fundamental impasse of being is at work in its structuring (as being). It is important, however, to stress the following: by insisting that the Lacanian concept of the sexual is not simply about any kind of sexual *content* (or sexual practice) we are in no way aiming at its "purification," trying to produce something like its pure form or pure (philosophical) idea, and hence making it philosophically more acceptable. The point is that beyond all sexual content and practices the sexual is not a pure form, but refers instead to the *absence of this form* as that which curves and defines the space of the sexual. In other words, this is an "absence" or a negativity that has important consequences for the field structured around it. How do we understand this?

The paradoxical status of sex is the opposite of, say, the status of unicorns: it is not about an entity that is nowhere to be found empirically, although we know exactly what it would look like if it were found empirically; rather, the opposite: empirically, there is no doubt that sex exists (and we are pretty well able to recognize, "identify" it); what seems to be missing—to put this in Platonic terms—is the Idea of sex, its essence: what exactly do we recognize when we say "this is sex"? Plato went so far as to say that even the lowest things, like mud and dirt, have their corresponding ideas (ideal essences), but what about sex? Is there an Idea, a pure form, of sex? The answer seems to be negative. And this is not because sex would be situated even "lower" on the chain of being than mud or dirt, but for some other reason. Presenting sex as low and "dirty" is already a response, a "solution" to its more fundamental scandal—namely, that we don't even know what it *is*. I have already insisted on this point: the embarrassment at and covering up of sexuality, as well as its controlling and regulating, should not be taken as self-explanatory, that is, as explained by the "traditional" cultural ban on sexuality, but rather the other way around: this ban should be explained by an ontological lapse involved in the sexual as sexual. The cause of embarrassment in sexuality is not simply something which is there, on display in it, but on the contrary, something that is not there—something which, if it existed, would determine what sex actually is, and name what is "sexual" about sex. Sex is all around, but we don't seem to know what exactly it is. We could perhaps go so far as to say: when—in the human realm—we come across something and have absolutely no clue what it is, we can be pretty certain that it "has to do with sex." This formula is not meant to be ironic. Il n'y a de sexe que de ce qui cloche: there is sex only in something that does not work.

In this precise sense culture is not simply a mask/veil of the sexual, it is the mask or, rather, a stand-in for something in the sexual which "is not." And it is also in this precise (indirect) sense that culture, civilization, is— as the classical Freudian stance goes—sexually driven, "motivated." It is not driven by that in the sexual which is, but rather by that which is not.

That in the sexual which is not is the relation: there is no sexual relation. This famous Lacanian claim is often understood too hastily as a learned and clever-sounding formulation of something that people, poems, litera- ture, films have always known and kept repeating in different ways: "(last- ing) true love is impossible," "love is mostly unhappy," "Men are from Mars, women are from Venus," "relationships don't work," "there are only series of (missed) encounters," "there are only atomized particles." ... It is easy to show where this kind of understanding moves too quickly and overrides, covers up, the Real expressed by Lacan's formula. What it does is immediately move to ontologize the non-relation(ship). And so we exclaim: "But of course, there is no sexual relation(ship)! This explains it all (and especially the history of our love life)." The fundamental ontological category, "being as being," is the non-relation, and this is why we are where we are!

In this way the non-relation is thus (wrongly) understood as the ultimate truth, the ultimate code or formula of reality. This truth is admittedly not very pleasant, but that is how it is, and at least we can understand why things are as they are. And it seems to make a lot of sense—compared to, for example, the formula produced by the superpowerful computer in Douglas Adams's famous novel The Hitchhiker's Guide to the Galaxy. After thousands and thousands of years of processing the question "What is the meaning of life?," the com- puter finally comes up with the answer, which is: 42. So—compared with this, Lacan's formula is literally bursting with sense or, more precisely, with the capacity to make sense of our miseries.

In this "understanding," we are thus led to conclude that the non-relation is the cause of the oddities and difficulties within all concrete relationships.

More precisely: the ontologically stated non-relation is seen in this perspective as the obstacle to the formation of any "successful" concrete, empirical relationship. Lacan's point, however, is paradoxically almost the opposite: it is only the inexistence of the relation that opens up the space for relationships and ties as we know them. In Lacan's own words: "the absence of the relation does of course not prevent the tie (la liaison), far from it—it dictates its conditions" (Lacan 2011, 19). The non-relation gives, dictates the conditions of, what ties us, which is to say that it is not a simple, indifferent absence, but an absence that curves and determines the structure with which it appears. The non-relation is not the opposite of the relationship, it is the inherent (il)logic (a fundamental "antagonism") of the relationships that are possible and existing.[2]

This represents a new and original conceptual model of the discursive space as generated out of, and around, a missing link in the ontological chain of its own reality. Biased by its constitutive negativity, this structure is always more or less than what it is, that is to say, more or less than the sum of its elements. Moreover, the causal link between these (signifying) elements is determined by what appears at the place of this negativity as both heterogeneous to and inseparable from the signifying order: the impossible substance of enjoyment, conceptualized by Lacan in terms of the (partial) object a. Object a is not a sexual object. Rather, it is a-sexual. It is the objective counterpart of the non-relation (we could say that it is non-relation as object). Yet it is also what is at work in all forming of ties, in the very structuring of (discursive) being qua being. With this in mind it is more than a pun, a play on words, to suggest that what follows from this Lacanian conceptualizations is an "object-disoriented ontology." If there is an ontology that follows from psychoanalytic (Lacanian) theory, this can only be an ontology as "disoriented" by what he calls the object a.

So, again, what is most valuable in the Freudo-Lacanian concept of sexuality is that it introduces a conceptual model of thinking the non-relation as dictating the conditions of different kinds of ties, including social ties (or discourses).[3]

It is in this precise sense that one could reaffirm the well-known slogan "the sexual is political" and give it a new, more radical meaning. "The sexual is political" not in the sense of sexuality as a realm of being where political struggles also take place, but in the sense that a true emancipatory politics can be thought only on the ground of an "object-disoriented ontology" as sketched above—that is, an ontology that pursues not simply being qua being, but the crack (the Real, the antagonism) that haunts being from within, informs it.

In what follows I will develop this with reference to an example which will help us explore and articulate more closely what is at stake in these claims.

The example is that of a most peculiar encounter between sexuality and politics as staged in an ingenious text by the Russian Marxist author Andrei Platonov, "The Anti-Sexus," situated at the very heart of the twentieth century's discussions of a possible emancipatory politics.

THE ANTI-SEXUS

In his introduction to the recent English (re)publication of Andrei Platonov's "The Anti-Sexus," Aaron Schuster made the following observation:

> If part of the twentieth century's revolutionary program to create a radically new social relation and a New Man was the liberation of sexuality, this aspiration was marked by a fundamental ambiguity: Is it sexuality that is to be liberated, delivered from moral prejudices and legal prohibitions, so that the drives are allowed a more open and fluid expression, or is humanity to be liberated from sexuality, finally freed from its obscure dependencies and tyrannical constraints? Will the revolution bring an efflorescence of libidinal energy or, seeing it as a dangerous distraction to the arduous task of building a new world, demand its suppression? In a word, is sexuality the object of or the obstacle to emancipation? (Schuster 2013, 42)

Schuster is quite right to suggest that this may be a mistaken alternative, in the sense that it misses something crucial about the psychoanalytic take on sexuality—as well as, we may add, about its take on emancipation. Whereas emancipation is most often conceived in terms of freeing ourselves from the (social) non-relation—or as approaching the Ideal of the Relation, even if it is unattainable—Lacan presents us with a very different perspective. The aim to abolish the non-relation (and to replace it with a Relation) is, rather, the trade- mark of all social repression. Sexual difference and the oppression of women are very good examples of this. The most oppressive societies have always been those which axiomatically proclaimed (enforced) the existence of the sexual relation: a "harmonious" relation presupposes an exact definition of essences (involved in this relation) and of roles pertaining to them. If there is to be a relation, women need to be such and such. A woman who *doesn't know her place* is a menace to the image of the relation (as a totality of two elements that complement each other, for example, or as any other kind of "cosmic order"). To this psychoanalysis does not respond by saying that woman is in fact something *other* than what these oppressive orders make her out to be, but with a very different, and much more powerful, claim: Woman does not exist. (We shall return to this later on, in our discussion of the sexual difference or divide.)

If we look at the history of political (and class) oppression, we can also see how the enforced idea of a "harmonious" system or social organism has always been accompanied by the most brutal forms of exclusion and oppression. The (Lacanian) point, however, is not simply something like: "Let's acknowledge the impossible (the non-relation), and instead of trying to 'force' it, rather, put up with it." This, indeed, is the official ideology of the contemporary "secular" form of social order and domination, which has abandoned the idea of a (harmonious) totality to the advantage of the idea of a non-totalizable multiplicity of singularities forming a "democratic" network. In this sense it may even seem that the non-relation is the dominant ideology of "capitalist democracies." We are all conceived as (more or less precious) singularities, "elementary particles," trying to make our voices heard in a complex, non-totalizable social network. There is no predetermined (social) relation, everything is negotiable, depending on us and on concrete circumstances. This, however, is very different from what Lacan's non-relation claim aims at. Namely: the (acknowledged) absence of the relation does not leave us with a pure pluralistic neutrality of (social) being. This kind of acknowledging of the non-relation does not really acknowledge it. What the (Lacanian) non-relation means is precisely that there is no neutrality of (social) being. At its most fundamental level, (social) being is already biased. The non-relation is not a simple absence of relation, but refers to a constitutive curving or bias of the discursive space—the latter is "biased" by the missing element of the relation. In this sense, to conceive democracy, for example, as a more or less successful negotiation between elements of a fundamentally neutral social being is to overlook—indeed, to repress—this consequential negativity, operative at the very core of the social order. It is in fact just another form of the narrative of the relation, which becomes quite clear if we think about how the political and economic ontology of the non-totalizable multiplicity of neutral singularities is usually accompanied by the idea of some kind of self-regulation. "The invisible hand of the market" is the showcase example of this.

For Lacan, the non-relation is a priori in the precise sense that it appears with every empirical relation as inherent to its structure, and not as its other. The choice is never that between relation and non-relation, but between different kinds of relations (bonds) that are being formed in the discursive space curved by the non-relation. The non-relation does not mean that there is no (fixed, predetermined) relation between particular elements, but refers to a declination, a twist in these elements themselves: "in themselves" these elements already bear the mark of the non-relation (and this mark is the surplus-enjoyment adhering to them). Acknowledging the non-relation does not mean accepting "the impossible" (as something that cannot be done), but seeing how it adheres to all things possible, how it in-forms them, what kind of antagonism it perpetuates in each concrete case, and how. This is the kind of acknowledgment that—far from closing it—only opens up the space of political invention and intervention.

But let us return to the "The Anti-Sexus" and to how it can help us see and define the core of the problem. So, what is this text? To sum it up, I will rely once more on Schuster's presentation:

In 1926, Russian Marxist author Andrei Platonov composed The Anti-Sexus, a remarkable text which remained, like so many of his other writings, unpublished during his lifetime. The work is a fictional brochure, issued by the company Berkman, Chateloy, and Son, Ltd. and "translated" from French by Platonov, that advertised an electromagnetic instrument promising to relieve sexual urges in an efficient and hygienic manner. The device, available in both male and female models, had a special regulator for the duration of pleasure and could be fitted for either personal or collective use. The purported occasion for the pamphlet was the company's expansion into the Soviet market after its success in many other parts of the world. The brochure includes a statement touting the virtues of the "Anti-Sexus" and the company's mission to "abolish the sexual savagery of mankind," and is followed by testimonials by a number of illustrious figures, from Henry Ford and Oswald Spengler to Gandhi and Mussolini. The Anti-Sexus, we are told, has many benefits and applications: it is perfect for maintaining soldiers' morale during wartime, for improving the efficiency of factory workers, for taming restless natives in the colonies. It also fosters true friendship and human understanding by taking sexual folly out of the social equation. The "translator" has added a critical preface where he condemns the cynicism and vulgarity of the enterprise, even while praising the pamphlet's writerly merits. He explains that the reason he decided to publish the text was to openly reveal the bourgeoisie's moral bankruptcy. No Bolshevik can read this capitalist drivel without a hearty laugh. The Anti-Sexus thus advertises itself as the surest form of "contra-'antisexual' agitprop." (Schuster 2013, 42–45)

We will not go into the (very interesting) question of where Platonov stands in this debate, staged as it is by him in a multilayered and multigenre way, in which a text of literary fiction is presented as a *translation* of an advertising *pamphlet* accompanied by *comments* by prominent men (yes, they are all men) and by a critical *introduction* from the alleged "translator." We will simply take the text at face value, and start by interrogating the presuppositions and par-adoxes of the device (called the Anti-Sexus) advertised and discussed in the alleged pamphlet.

These are the presuppositions of the Anti-Sexus device: Sexuality is prob-lematic because it involves the Other who, as everybody knows, is utterly unpredictable, unreliable (has her own will, caprices, indispositions...) or simply unavailable. On the other hand, and *at the same time*, our relations with others are complicated and conflict-ridden because expectations and demands concerning sex are always in the air, complicating things: sex stands in the way of good social relations. This is the double quandary presumably resolved by the Anti-Sexus device, which is claimed to be able to isolate, extirpate what is sexual about enjoyment, from all other pleasures and relations in which it appears—to distillate, as it were, the pure essence of sex (and then administer it in just the right dosages). In this way, the Anti-Sexus provides an "Other-free" enjoyment (enjoyment free of the Other) and at the same time makes it possible for us to relate to others in a really meaningful way: to create real, lasting bonds (pure spiritual friendship).

It is clear that two operations are at stake here, or two aims: on the one hand, the aim is to extract sex from the Other; on the other hand, it is to exempt the Other from sex. In this way we get two separate entities: as the result of the first operation, we get a sexless Other (to whom one can now relate in a friendly and non-problematic way); as the result of the second operation, we get a pure substance of sex, which we can enjoy directly whenever we want to.

The Anti-Sexus is said to accomplish both things:

> We have been called upon to solve the global human problem of sex and the soul. Our company has transformed sexual feeling from a crude elemental urge to an ennobling mechanism, we have given the world moral behavior. We have removed the element of sex from human relationships and cleared the way for pure spiritual friendship.
>
> Still, keeping in mind the high-value instant pleasure that necessarily accompanies contact of the sexes, we have endowed our instrument with a construction affording a minimum of three times this pleasure, as compared to the loveliest of women used at length by a prisoner recently released after ten years in strict isolation. (Platonov 2013, 50)

As much as we can be tempted to laugh here, this addresses a problem that has been all but constantly raised in modern debates concerning the possible (and radical) emancipation of humankind: *the crucial obstacle to global human emancipation is humanity* ("human nature") itself. Human emancipation is actually emancipation from the human. Human nature is the weak link in the project of social emancipation. In this line of thought we usually get a harder and a softer mode of resolving this dilemma: either to build a New Man, or to "canalize" the disruptive factor of humanity, and "satisfy" it in a way that cannot interfere with building and maintaining the social Relation.[4]

The proposition of the Anti-Sexus is to canalize the disruptive element. But this is the problem: can this "disruptive element" really be thought of in terms of an *element*, that is, in terms of something that one can define, circumscribe, isolate? The answer seems to be no, and this is most evident in the way in which the basic operation of the Anti-Sexus immediately falls into two different operations: extracting, removing sex from the Other, and exempting, removing the Other from sex. Not much is said about how the first is done; the device basically provides the method of the second. It exempts the Other from sexual pleasure, and the idea is, it would seem, that this automatically accomplishes the other task as well: it extracts, removes sex from the Other, or produces a sexless Other, ready to form spiritual bonds with me. Since the sexual needs of the Other are always perfectly satisfied, she or he becomes sexless (sex is not a player in the relationship between people). This, of course, is a strange presupposition, to say the least. The Other is sexless if he or she "is being masturbated" most of the time.

And here we come to the very "matheme" of the Anti-Sexus device, which I propose to formulate as follows: "to make oneself masturbated," "*se faire masturber*"—to paraphrase the grammatical form used by Lacan in his conceptualization of the drive.[5] In order to properly conceptualize the drive as something that escapes the active/passive opposition, Lacan proposes a formula that introduces something active at the very heart of passivity, and vice versa. In the case of the scopic drive, for example, he dismantles what looks like reversal(s) between *seeing* and *being seen* with the formulation *making oneself seen*. In this sense the Anti-Sexus and its formula ("to make oneself masturbated") could be said to provide the formula of the nonexistent "sexual drive." We saw how its task is actually twofold and twisted: in order to remove enjoyment from the Other, one has to remove the Other from enjoyment. This suggests in fact that enjoyment and the Other are structured like a matryoshka: enjoyment is "in" the Other, but when we look "in" the enjoyment, there is also the Other "in" it, and so on....Enjoyment is in the Other, and the Other is in enjoyment. —This is perhaps the most concise formulation of the structure of the non-relation, the non-relation between the subject and the Other. If enjoyment is what disturbs this relation, it does so not simply by coming *between* them (and hence holding them apart), but rather by *implicating*, placing them one in the other.

Let us take a moment here and look more closely at both sides of this configuration.

What we have on the one hand is this: all enjoyment already presupposes the Other, regardless of whether we "get it" with the help of the "real other" (another person) or not. This is Lacan's fundamental point. Even the most solitary enjoyment presupposes the structure of the Other. This is also why, the more we try to get rid of the Other and become utterly self-dependent, the more we are bound to find something radically heterogeneous ("Other") at the very heart of our most intimate enjoyment. There is no enjoyment without the Other, because all enjoyment originates at the place of the Other (as the locus of the signifiers). Our innermost enjoyment can occur only at that "extimate" place. (And this is not the same as saying that enjoyment is *mediated* by the Other, or that we "need" the Other in order to enjoy.) It is of the utmost importance to grasp that the radical heterogeneity, incommensurability, and antagonism between the signifier and enjoyment is not due to their heterogeneous origins (for example, that one comes from the body and the other from the symbolic order), but on the contrary to the fact that they *originate at the same place.* The Other is *both* the locus of the signifier *and* the locus of enjoyment (mine, as well as the enjoyment of the Other).

On the other hand (and as we saw in chapter 1), what we find, for example, at the very heart of the most sex-free, spiritual (Christian) love is a proliferation of partial objects and their enjoyment. It is not pure enjoyment, "enjoyment for the sake of enjoyment," that is being banned in this discourse; what is banned, or repressed, is the link between enjoyment and sexuality.

But why exactly? Because this link exposes the non-relation at *the very heart* of every relation. Like all religions, Christianity presupposes and enforces the Relation. The idea of a "nonsexual sexual enjoyment" that we find here is actually the same as the one at work in the Anti-Sexus device. What is needed for the Relation to exist is a "sexless sex," or an "otherless Other" (an Other free of otherness).

This, then, is the double paradox that we are trying to formulate: if we remove the Other from enjoyment, we find the Other at the very heart of the most autofocused, masturbatory enjoyment. On the other hand: if we remove enjoyment from the Other, we find enjoyment at the very heart of the (most spiritual) bond with the Other. The Other and enjoyment are "extimately" related. This is why, in order to remove enjoyment from the Other, a second operation is immediately called for: that of removing the Other from enjoyment. The two "elements" imply each other, each carries the other "in" itself, and this is what twists what may look like a symmetry (or relation) in a way that resembles some of Escher's drawings of impossible objects.

"THE INVISIBLE 'HANDJOB' OF THE MARKET"

Lacan's point is that, since it is one with the discursive order, the non-relation is at work in all forms of social bond; it is not limited to the "sphere of love." (The latter is, rather, distinguished by the fact that in its field it actually happens, from time to time, that the relation "stops not being written.") And his further point is that the social relations of power—domination, exploitation, discrimination—are first and foremost *forms of exploitation of the non-relation.*

This is a delicate point, for it seems to contradict a point made earlier: namely, that the most authoritarian social orders are those which aim at freeing the social from the non-relation, that is to say, social orders built in the name of the Relation. Yet this is not necessarily in contradiction with exploiting the non-relation. Perhaps we even find here a good way of distinguishing between the abolition of the non-relation as emancipatory project, and what we may call "narratives of the Relation" which are actually in the service of the most vicious (social and economic) *exploitation of the non-relation.* Abolition of the non-relation has been in fact the way in which the authentic revolutionary projects of the twentieth century often understood the path to radical emancipation. The catastrophic results of this kind of politics were inherent in the very honesty of the will to abolish the non-relation. The modus operandi of engineering a New order (and a New man) has been that of exposing the non-relation and attempting to force it out of the social equation, by all possible means. And this is very different, in its logic, from what we may call the exploitation and segregation of people by presenting a given form of social antagonism (non-relation) as the ultimate Relation, supposedly protecting us from the utter Chaos of the non-relation. In this way, social injustice directly translates into a higher Justice. At work here is not a crazy attempt to abolish the non-relation as the fundamental negativity, but *disavowing* it while at the same time *appropriating* it as the generic (and productive) point of social power. This is a truly political lesson of psychoanalysis: Power—and particularly modern forms of power—works by first appropriating a fundamental negativity of the symbolic order, its constitutive non-relation, while building it into a narrative of a higher Relation. This is what constitutes, puts into place and perpetuates, the relations of domination. And the actual, concrete exploitation is based on, made possible (and fueled) by, this appropriation, this "privatization of the negative." This is what distinguishes—to take the famous Brechtian example—the robbing of a bank (common theft) from the founding of a bank (a double theft which appropriates the very lever of production and its exploitation).

Nowhere is this more evident than in the case of capitalism, which starts off with two revolutionary ideas: "the economic Relation does not exist" and "the non-relation could be very profitable." The first idea corresponds to the eighteenth-century economists, led by Adam Smith, putting into question the previous "mercantile" doctrine and belief that the amount of the world's wealth remained constant and that a nation could increase its wealth only at the expense of another nation. This is the image of a "closed" totality in which the relation ensures the visibility of the difference (in wealth): if you want more, you have to take it from somewhere, so someone else has to lose. The relation is that of subordination (of the weak to the powerful), but it is still a relation. The new economic idea undermines this (totality-based) relation, while at the same time prizing the productivity of the newly discovered non-relation. The world's wealth can also increase "by itself," with the Industrial Revolution and the new organization of labor being the primary sources and carriers of this increase. I am deliberately putting this in the crudest and most simple terms, so as to expose the most salient structural traits of this shift. What is the fundamental "discovery" of capitalism? That non-relation is profitable, that it is the ultimate source of growth and profit. And with this came the idea that, this being so, there is no reason why everybody couldn't profit from it. This is how we got the narrative of a new, higher Relation, the foundational myth of modern capitalism, known as "the invisible hand of the market."

Adam Smith's "capital" idea starts out from positing a social non-relation as a fundamental state also on another level: as elements of social order, individuals are driven by egotistic drives and the pursuit of self-interest. But out of these purely egotistic pursuits grows a society of an optimal general welfare and justice. It is precisely by ruthlessly pursuing one's own interest that one promotes the good of society as a whole, and much more efficiently so than when one sets off to promote it directly. As Smith puts it in a famous quote from The Wealth of Nations: "It is not from the benevolence of the butcher, the brewer or the baker, that we expect our dinner, but from their regard to their own self- interest. We address ourselves, not to their humanity but to their self-love, and never talk to them of our own necessities but of their advantages" (Smith 2005, 30).

What is interesting about this idea in the context of our previous discussion is how it takes a first step in the right direction and then stops short. To put it in the terms we were using earlier, the idea is that what we find at the very core of the most selfish individual enjoyment is actually the Other (looking after a general welfare). What is missing is the next step: and what we find, at the same time, at the core of this Other, is a most "masturbatory" self-enjoyment. Adam Smith's mistake is not that he saw the dimension of the Other possibly at work in the most selfish pursuits of individual interests—all in all, this thesis is not simply wrong: we never do just what we think we are doing and what we intend to do (this is even a fundamental lesson of both Hegel and Lacan). His mistake was that he did not follow this logic to the end: he failed to see where and how the Other and its invisible hand *also* do not do only what they think they are doing.... This is what becomes obvious with every economic crisis, and became overwhelmingly clear with the last one: left to itself, the market (the Other) is bound to discover "solitary enjoyment." At some point in his comments on Platonov's "Anti-Sexus," Schuster uses the expression: "the invisible 'handjob' of the market," which I am borrowing here, since one could hardly find a better way of putting what I am trying to articulate. The invisible hand of the market, supposedly looking after general welfare and justice, is always also, and already, the invisible handjob of the market, putting most of the wealth decidedly out of common reach.

Adam Smith's idea could indeed be formulated in these terms: Let's make the non-relation work for everybody's profit. And one could hardly deny the fact that what we consider as wealth has increased in absolute (and not only relative) terms since the eighteenth century. Or, as we often hear, that everybody, even the poorest, is living better than two centuries ago. Yet the price of this modern economic higher Relation is, again, that the differences (between rich and poor) are also exponentially greater, fed by the non-relation in its "higher" form.

Why is the non-relation so productive and profitable? Marx saw it perfectly: in order for the non-relation to be economically productive and profitable, it has to be built into the very mode of production. He situated this at the precise "structural" point when labor appeared on the market as yet another commodity for sale. This is a key point in what he analyzes as "the transformation of money into capital." To put it very simply: what makes the products (namely, labor power) also appears with them on the market as one of the products, objects for sale. This paradoxical redoubling corresponds to the point of structural negativity and its appropriation as the locus of the market's "miraculous" productivity. The money-owner finds on the market a commodity whose use value possesses the peculiar property of being a source of value, and whose actual consumption is a creation of value. This is why it is too simple to say that what the capitalists have "more of," they have "stolen" from the workers. This kind of claim still presupposes the old, "closed," relation-based economy.... What capital exploits is the point of negativity ("entropy") of the social order, with the workers situated at this precise point. Capitalists are not so much "stealing" from the workers as employing them to make the negativity/entropy of the system work for them, the capitalists. Or, in other words: "they are making themselves enriched."

This, then, is what Marx recognized as the concrete structural point of the non-relation in capitalism, serving as the condition of its type of production and exploitation. Labor power as commodity is the point that marks the constitutive negativity, gap, of this system: the point where one thing immediately falls into another (use value into source of value). Labor is a product among other products, yet it is not exactly like other products: where other products have a use value (and hence a substance of value), this particular commodity "leaps over" or "lapses" to the source of value. The use value of this commodity is to be the source of value of (other) commodities. It has no "substance" of its own. This could also be put in a formula: "The Worker does not exist." What exists—and must exist—is the person whose work is sold and bought. This is why it is essential, according to Marx, that the person working does not sell himself (his person), "converting himself from a free man to a slave, from an owner of commodity into a commodity. He must constantly treat his labor-power as his own property, his own commodity" (Marx 1990, 271). This also shows how the usual humanist complaints about how, in capitalism, "we are all just commodities" miss the point: if we were indeed just commodities, capitalism would not work; we need to be free persons selling our labor power as our property, our commodity.

The Marxian concept of the proletariat could be seen precisely as formulating the fact that, in capitalism, the Worker doesn't exist (a Worker that existed would actually be a slave). This is why the proletariat is not simply one of the social classes, but rather names the point of the *concrete consti-tutive negativity*[6] in capitalism, the point of the non-relation obfuscated and exploited by it. The proletariat is not the sum of all workers, it is the concept that names the symptomatic point of this system, its disavowed and exploited negativity. And this general Marxian idea has lost none of its pertinence today.

In conclusion, we can return to the invisible hand, its other side and its criticism: is it enough to claim that it does not exist, and to try to put in its place a better, truly operative Other? As a matter of fact, this is precisely the theoretical question that we see today emerging on the left (for example, with Thomas Piketty's work): is it tenable to play one's cards on the side of distribution? In other words, is there a way in which we could make the non-relation-based profit *really* profitable for all (eliminate its "handjob" aspect, as it were)? Can we maintain the profitable side of the non-relation while keep-ing its negative side under control (by means of different social correctives and regulations concerning the distribution of wealth)?

CHAPTER 3

CONTRADICTIONS THAT MATTER

SEX OR GENDER?

Let us recapitulate some of the important points made so far, which will orient us in our further discussion. One of the founding gestures of psychoanalysis was to cut short the discussion of sexuality as a moral question by relating it to an epistemological difficulty, with immanent ontological relevance. What, in fact, is sexuality? Far from chaining humanity to its animal or natural heritage, sexuality is the problematic territory of being that seems to throw us out of joint, disorient us, and make us indulge in things characteristic of human society (politics, art, science, love, religion...). In his early work Freud still played with the simple idea of casting sexuality as the hidden motive: repressed sexuality resurfaces as the driving force behind all kinds of highly spiritual human creations, as well as horrors. Later, he put it in a different perspective, additionally fortified by Lacan and his "return to Freud": if sexuality is so closely related to the unconscious and to mechanisms of repression, the reason is not its moral controversy, but its paradoxical ontological status, manifesting itself as an epistemological problem, or an epistemological limit. Moral issues surrounding sexuality (its concealment and shame, its oppression, its codification and regulation, its penalization, as well as its liberation, its revealing, displaying and endlessly discussing) have their origin in sexuality as an ontological problem. Sexuality is the paradigm of research and exploration, not in the sense of the reduction to the last instance but, on the contrary, because it brutally introduces us to the lack of the last instance. It is precisely this lack of the last instance that becomes the place of thought, including the most speculative (metaphysical) thinking. And it is no coincidence that the discussion of sexual difference in psychoanalysis, in its most venerable tradition, often sounds or reads like "high mathematics": formulas, logical paradoxes, complicated formulations, and counterintuitive theses. Theses concerning sexuality are in fact the most speculative (or "philosophical") part of psychoanalytic theory. It is also no coincidence that the shift from considering sexuality as a moral issue to focusing on its problematic ontological and epistemological status casts sexuality (and particularly sexual difference) as an immediate *political* problem. Not a cultural problem, not a problem of identity, but a political problem. Not a problem of "human rights," but a problem of political rights. At its core, feminism has always been a political movement. This is precisely what contemporary ideology tries to make us forget (or else to make us dismiss, precisely *because* it was political). We get images of "hysterical," "fanatical," "masculine," "wild," "ideological" suffragettes as opposed to "calm," "composed" women who see themselves as human beings with specific qualities and an *identity*, and try to democratically affirm it; women who would start by saying, "I'm not a feminist, I just…" True feminism depends on positing sexual difference as a political problem, and hence on situating it in the context of social antagonism and of emancipatory struggle. Feminism did not start from trying to affirm some other, female identity (and its rights), but from the fact that roughly half of the human race, referred to as "women," was nonexistent in a political sense. It is this nonexistence, this political invisibility, which actually functioned as a *homogeneity* of the political space, that feminism transformed into a split, a division, which concerns *all* (hence its political dimension). In this context it is essential that at stake in this gesture is not a political affirmation of some independently existing ontological divide (between "men" and "women"), but something that first constitutes sexual difference as difference or divide. And it does so by forcing us to think of it as a division, a split of *the same world*. The traditional division between masculine and feminine worlds (domains, spheres: for example, public/private) actually does not see sexual difference as difference, but as a question of belonging to two separate worlds, which are "different" from a neutral bird's-eye description, but otherwise coexist as integral parts in the hierarchy of a higher cosmic order, the wholeness and unity of which is in no way threatened by this "difference." These are parts that "know their place." And feminism (as a political movement) puts in question, and breaks, precisely this unity of the world, based on massive suppression, subordination, and exclusion. Once again: this exclusion is not an exclusion of female identity; on the contrary, the mythology of female identity is precisely what has made this exclusion possible, and what sustains it. The theme of "female identity" sustains the difference and exclusion on the prepolitical level, on the level of belonging to two different worlds. In this sense, (emancipatory) politics begins with "loss of identity," and there is nothing deplorable in this loss. Preachers of traditional values usually propagate the political exclusion of women precisely by evoking their (specific) identity. They believe that the Woman exists, and they need Her to exist. Is the right response to this to fill the "Woman" up with different content and to promote her as the Other voice, the voice of alterity, which also needs to be heard and affirmed? No: the political explosiveness of "the woman question" does not lie in any specificity or positive characteristics of women, but in its capacity to inscribe the problem of division and difference into the world the homogeneity of which is based on exclusion. This exclusion—and this point is absolutely crucial—is not simply the exclusion of the other side, or half, but above all the exclusion ("repression") of the split (social antagonism) as such; it is the erasing of a social antagonism. Its reappearance (in the form of feminist struggle) is the appearance of the social division in the pure state, and this is what makes it political, and politically explosive.

Sexual difference is a singular kind of difference, because it starts out not as difference between different identities, but as an ontological impossibility (implied in sexuality) which only opens up the space of the social (where identities are also generated). This ontologically determinative negativity involved in the concept of sexual difference is precisely what is lost with the replacement of this concept with that of "gender differences." As Joan Copjec forcefully put it:

> The psychoanalytic category of sexual difference was from this date [the mid-1980s] deemed suspect and largely forsaken in favor of the neutered category of gender. Yes, neutered. I insist on this because it is specifically the sex of sexual difference that dropped out when this term was replaced by gender. Gender theory performed one major feat: it removed the sex from sex. For while gender theorists continued to speak of sexual practices, they ceased to question what sex or sexuality is; in brief, sex was no longer the subject of an ontological inquiry and reverted instead to being what it was in common parlance: some vague sort of distinction, but basically a secondary characteristic (when applied to the subject), a qualifier added to others, or (when applied to an act) something a bit naughty. (Copjec 2012, 31)

If we want to avoid this move, the crucial question becomes: What exactly does the insistence on sex (and sexual difference) as the subject of an ontological inquiry amount to?

To even suggest discussing sexual difference as an ontological question might induce—not without justification—strong reluctance, the objection that this discussion would achieve nothing new. Traditional ontologies and traditional cosmologies were strongly reliant on sexual difference, taking it as their very founding, or structuring, principle. Yin–yang, water–fire, earth–sun, matter–form, active–passive—this kind of (often explicitly sexualized) opposition was used as the organizing principle of these ontologies and/or cosmologies, as well as of the sciences—astronomy, for example—based on them. And this is how Lacan could say: "primitive science is a sort of sexual technique."[1] At some point in history, one generally associated with the Galilean revolution in science and its aftermath, both science and philosophy broke with this tradition. And if there is a simple and most general way of saying what characterizes modern science and modern philosophy, it could be phrased precisely in terms of the "desexualization" of reality, of abandoning sexual difference, in more or less explicit form, as the organizing principle of reality, meant or used to provide its coherence and intelligibility.

The reasons why feminism and gender studies find these ontologizations of sexual difference highly problematic are obvious. Fortified on the ontological level, sexual difference is strongly anchored in essentialism—it becomes a combinatory game of the essences of masculinity and femininity. Such that, to put it in contemporary gender studies parlance, the social production of norms and their subsequent descriptions finds a ready-made ontological division, ready to essentialize "masculinity" and "femininity" immediately. Traditional ontology was thus always also a machine for producing "masculine" and "feminine" essences, or, more precisely, for grounding these essences in being.

When modern science broke with this ontology, it also mostly broke with ontology *tout court*. (Modern) science is not ontology; it neither pretends to make ontological claims nor, from a critical perspective on science, recognizes that it is nevertheless making them.

Perhaps more surprisingly, modern philosophy also mostly broke not only with traditional ontology but also with ontology *tout court*. Immanuel Kant is the name most strongly associated with this break: If one can have no knowledge about things in themselves, the classical ontological question of being *qua* being seems to lose its ground.[2] It is a fact, however, that the ontological debate, after a considerable time of withdrawal from the foreground of the philosophical (theoretical) stage—and, perhaps even more importantly, of not appealing to the general interest—is now making a massive "return" to this stage, with an outburst of "new ontologies." To be sure, these are diverse and sometimes very different philosophical projects. But it is safe to say that for none of them does sexual difference (in any form) play any part in their ontological considerations.

Since we are debating psychoanalysis and sexual difference, implicating Freud and Lacan in the discussion of the ontological dimension of sexual difference might look like the summit of possible oddities. For it seems not only to go against the numerous and outstanding efforts the defenders of psychoanalysis have, for decades, invested in showing the incompatibility of psychoanalysis with any kind of sexual essentialism; it is also contrary to what both Freud and Lacan thought and said about ontology. In view of the desexualization of reality that occurred with the Galilean revolution in science mentioned above, psychoanalysis (at least in its Freudian-Lacanian vein) is far from lamenting this. Its diagnosis of Western civilization is not one of the "forgetting of the sexual," and it does not see itself as something that will bring the sexual coloring of the universe back into focus again, as if reenchanting it (sexually). On the contrary, it sees itself (and its "object") as strictly coextensive with the move of desexualization.

> [Psychoanalysis] proceeds from the same status as Science *itself*. It is engaged in the central lack in which the subject experiences itself as desire....It has nothing to forget [a reference, no doubt, to the Heideggerian "forgetting of Being"], for it implies no recognition of any substance on which it claims to operate, even that of sexuality. (Lacan 1987, 266)

I am not making this point, however, in order to argue that psychoanalysis is in fact much less centered on the sexual than is commonly assumed, or to promote the "culturalized version" of psychoanalysis. Rather, the sexual in psychoanalysis is something very different from the sense-making combinatory game—it is precisely something that disrupts this game and makes it impossible. What one needs to see and grasp, to begin with, is where the real divide runs here. Psychoanalysis is *both* coextensive with this desexualization of reality, in the sense of breaking with ontology and science as a sexual technique or sexual combinatory, *and* absolutely uncompromising when it comes to the sexual as the irreducible *Real* (not substance). There is no contradiction here, just as there is no contradiction in the opposite, Jungian "revisionist" stance, which articulates a total culturalization of the sexual (its transcription into cultural archetypes) while also maintaining the principle of ontological combinatory (of two fundamental principles, *yin* and *yang*). The lesson and the imperative of psychoanalysis is not "Let us devote all our attention to the sexual (meaning) as our ultimate horizon"; it is instead a reduction of sex and the sexual (which, in fact, has always been overloaded with meanings and interpretations) to the point of ontological inconsistency, which, *as such*, is irreducible.

Lacan's emphatic claim that psychoanalysis is *not* a new ontology (a sexual ontology, for example) is thus not something that we are going to contest. But we will also not take the stance according to which psychoanalysis simply does not (and would not) have anything to do with ontology. The stakes are much higher, and the psychoanalytic relationship to philosophy (as ontology) is much more interesting and intricate. Perhaps the best way of putting it would be to say that their non-relationship, implied in "psychoanalysis is not an ontology," is of the most intimate kind. I hope this statement will justify itself in what follows.

One of the conceptual deadlocks in simply emphasizing that gender is an entirely social, or cultural, construction is that it remains within the dichotomy nature/culture. Judith Butler saw this very clearly,[3] which is why her project radicalizes this theory by linking it to the theory of performativity. As opposed to expressivity, indicating a preexistence and independence of that which is being expressed, performativity refers in Butler's account to actions that create, so to speak, the essences that they express. Nothing here preexists: sociosymbolic practices of different discourses and their antagonisms create the very "essences," or phenomena, that they regulate. The time and the dynamics of repetition that this creation requires open up the only margin of freedom (to possibly change or influence this process). What differentiates this concept of performativity from the classical, linguistic one is precisely the element of time: it is not that the performative gesture creates a new reality immediately, that is, in the very act of being performed (like the performative utterance "I declare this session open"); rather, it refers to a process in which sociosymbolic constructions, by dint of repetition and reiteration, become nature—"only natural," as the saying goes. What is referred to as natural is the sedimentation of the discursive, and in this view the dialectics of nature and culture becomes the internal dialectics of culture. Culture both produces and regulates (what is referred to as) "nature." We are no longer dealing with two terms: sociosymbolic activity, and something on which it is performed; instead, we are dealing with something like an internal dialectics of the One (the discursive) that not only models things but also creates the things it models, which opens up a certain depth of field. Performativity is thus a kind of onto-logy of the discursive, responsible for both the *logos* and the *being* of things.

To a great extent, Lacanian psychoanalysis seems compatible with this account, and it is often presented as such. The primacy of the signifier and of the field of the Other, language as constitutive of reality and of the unconscious (including the dialectics of desire), the creationist aspect of the symbolic and its dialectics (with notions such as symbolic causality, symbolic efficiency, materiality of the signifier)…all of these (undisputed) claims notwithstanding, Lacan's position is irreducibly different from the performative ontology described above. In what way, exactly? And what is the status of the Real that Lacan insists upon when speaking of sexuality?

It is not simply that Lacan has to take into account and make room for the other, "vital" part of the psychoanalytic notions (such as the libido, the drive, the sexualized body), which would be defined as "real," as opposed to belonging to the symbolic. This kind of parlance, and the perspective it implies, are very misleading. Something else is at stake: taking the signifying order as his starting point, Lacan sees it as the locus of a fundamental split. While the signifying order creates its own space and the beings that populate it (which roughly corresponds to the space of performativity described above), *something else gets added to it*. It could be said that this something is parasitic on performative productivity; it is not produced by the signifying gesture, but together with and "on top of" it. It is inseparable from this gesture, but, unlike what we call discursive entities/beings, not created by it. It is neither a symbolic entity nor one constituted by the symbolic; rather, it is collateral for the symbolic. Moreover, it is not a being: it is discernible only as a (disruptive) effect within the symbolic field, its disturbance, its bias. In other words, the emergence of the signifier is not reducible to, or exhausted by, the symbolic. The signifier does not only produce a new, symbolic reality (including its own materiality, causality, and laws); it also "produces" the dimension that Lacan calls the Real, which is related to the points of structural impossibility/contradiction of symbolic reality itself. This is what irredeemably stains the symbolic, stains its supposed purity, and accounts for the fact that the symbolic game of pure differentiality is always a game with loaded dice. This is the very space, or dimension, that sustains the "vital" phenomena mentioned above (the libido or *jouissance*, the drive, the sexualized body) in their out-of-jointness with the symbolic.

So: the something produced by the signifier, in addition to what it produces as its field, magnetizes this field in a certain way. It is responsible for the fact that the symbolic field, or the field of the Other, is never neutral (or structured by pure differentality), but conflictual, asymmetrical, "not-all," ridden with a fundamental antagonism. In other words, the antagonism of the discursive field is not due to the fact that this field is always "composed" of multiple elements, or multiple multiples, competing among themselves and not properly unified; it refers to the very space in which these different multiples exist. Just as, for Marx, "class antagonism" is not simply conflict between different classes but the very principle of the constitution of class society, antagonism as such never simply exists *between* conflicting parties; it is the very structuring principle of this conflict, and of the elements involved in it.

Yet this account demands a further specification, which makes it slightly more complex. For we could ask: But how is it that the signifier "produces" something on top of what it produces as its (properly signifying) field? Why does this happen? And the answer (with which we come back to a crucial point that I have already introduced) is: because the signifying structure is coextensive with a gap.

> Discourse begins from the fact that there is a gap here....But, after all, nothing prevents us from saying that it is because discourse begins that the gap is produced. It is a matter of complete indifference toward the result. What is certain is that discourse is implied in the gap. (Lacan 2006b, 107)

This implication of discursivity and gap is a crucial point, or at least the point that I will take as crucial in my argument. Lacan's writing of it, with which we have become familiar, is this: $S(\cancel{A})$, referring to a constitutive lack in the Other. What I would like to emphasize is the dimension of something like virtual subtraction or "minus" involved in this notion. This emphasis allows us to say not only that the signifying order is inconsistent and incomplete, but, in a stronger and more paradoxical phrasing, that the signifying order emerges as already lacking one signifier, that it appears with the lack of a signifier "built into it," so to speak (a signifier which, if it existed, would be the "binary signifier"). In this precise sense the signifying order could be said to begin, not with One (nor with multiplicity), but with a "minus one"—and we shall return to this crucial point in more detail later on. It is in the place of this gap or negativity that appears the surplus-enjoyment which stains the signifying structure: the heterogeneous element pertaining to the signifying structure, yet irreducible to it.

We could also say: The emergence of the signifying order directly coincides with the non-emergence of one signifier, and this fact (this original minus one) leaves its trace in a particular feature/disturbance of the signifying system—enjoyment. So it is not so much that the signifier "produces" this surplus as that this surplus is the way in which the lack of the (binary) signifier exists within the discursive structure and marks it in certain determinable ways. It marks (and thus effectively "curves") it by sticking to a certain set (or chain) of other signifiers that relate in some way to this lack of the signifier. The way enjoyment relates to (or is linked to) the signifying order passes through what is missing in this order; it does not relate to it directly, but via its constitutive negativity (a minus one). This negativity is the Real of the junction between the (missing) signifier and enjoyment; and the conceptual name for this configuration in psychoanalysis is sexuality (or the sexual). Sexuality is coextensive with the effect of the signifying gap, at the place of which surplus-enjoyment emerges, on the rest of the signifying chain (including bodily erogenous zones which are certainly not independent of the signifying grid).

Sexuality is not some being that exists beyond the symbolic; it "exists" solely as the contradiction of the symbolic space that appears because of the constitutively missing signifier, and of what appears at its place (enjoyment).

It would thus be wrong to say that the signifier of the sexual is missing; the sexual is not some extradiscursive object lacking a signifier; rather, it is a direct consequence ("extension") of the missing of a signifier, that is, of the gap with which the signifying order emerges. This is why sexuality is neither something outside of the signifying order (which this order would strive to represent fully, but fail), nor does it have a signifier. To spell it out in full: human sexuality is the placeholder of the missing signifier. It is a mess, but it is a mess that actually compensates for the sexual relation as impossible (to be written). This, I believe, is a crucial reversal of the common perception that we need to make: the messiness of our sexuality is not a consequence or result of there being no sexual relation, it is not that our sexuality is messy because it is without a clear signifying rule; it emerges only from, and at the place of, this lack, and attempts to deal with it. Sexuality is not ravaged by, or disturbed, because of a gap cutting deep into its "tissue," it is, rather, the messy sewing up of this gap. Lacan actually says as much in a rather offhand remark in the Seminar…ou pire, but it is absolutely crucial: the four formulas known as the formulas of sexuation are his attempt to "fix that which makes up for [supplée à] what I have called the impossibility to write the sexual relation" (Lacan 2011, 138). In other words, sex is messy because it appears at the point of the breaking down of the signifying consistency, or logic (its point of impossibility), not because it is in itself illogical and messy: its messiness is the result of the attempt to invent a logic at the very point of the impasse of such logic. Its "irrationality" is the summit of its efforts to establish a sexual "rationale." This, at least, is how Lacan conceived of the formulas of sexuation: they (re)state the issue of sexuality and "sexual relations" as a logical problem (problem of the signifying logic) out of which it springs.

If we now return to the question of what all this implies in relation to ontology in general, and, more specifically, to the performative ontology of contemporary gender studies, we must start from the following crucial implication: Lacan is led to establish a difference between being and the Real. The Real is not a being, or a substance, but its deadlock, the point of its impossibility. It is inseparable from being, yet it is not being. One could say that for psychoanalysis, there is no being independent of language (or discourse)—which is why it often seems compatible with contemporary forms of nominalism. All being is symbolic; it is being in the Other. But with a crucial addition, which could be formulated as follows: there is only being in the symbolic—except that there is the Real. There "is" the Real, but this Real is no being. Yet it is not simply the outside of being; it is not something besides being, it is a convulsion, a stumbling block of the space of being. It exists only as the inherent contradiction of (symbolic) being. This, and nothing else, is at stake when psychoanalysis links sex with the Real. As Joan Copjec put it in her seminal text on these questions:

> When we speak of language's failure with respect to sex, we speak not of its falling short of a prediscursive object but of its falling into contradiction with itself. Sex coincides with this failure, this inevitable contradiction. Sex is, then, the impossibility of completing meaning, not (as Butler's historicist/deconstructionalist argument would have it) a meaning that is incomplete, instable. Or, the point is that sex is the structural incompleteness of language, not that sex is itself incomplete. (Copjec 1994, 206)

This conceiving of the Real as the point of the internal impossibility/contradiction of being is why Lacan holds the Real to be the bone in the throat of every ontology: in order to speak of "being *qua* being," one has to amputate something in being that is not being. That is to say, the Real is that which traditional ontology had to cut off in order to be able to speak of "being *qua* being." We arrive at being *qua* being only by subtracting, eradicating something from it. Being *qua* being is not some elementary given, but is already a result which presupposes another, previous step. And this step consists not in eradicating or suppressing some contradictive positivity, but in eradicating a specific, real negativity (contradiction as such). What gets lost here is the something in being that is less than being—and this something is precisely that which, while included in being, prevents it from being fully constituted *as being*.

And—to return to our previous discussion—this concept of the Real (as a crack in being) is precisely what is lost in translation when we pass from "sex" to "gender." It might seem paradoxical, but to some extent differences like form–matter, yin–yang, active–passive…belong to the same onto-logy as "gender" differences. Even when this onto-logy abandons the principle of complementarity and embraces that of gender multiplicity, this in no way affects the ontological status of entities called genders. They are said to *be*, or to exist, and emphatically so. (This "emphatically" seems to increase with numbers: one is usually timid in asserting the existence of two genders, but when it goes on to the multitude this timidity disappears, and their existence is firmly asserted.) If sexual difference is considered in terms of gender, it is made—at least in principle—compatible with the mechanisms of its full ontologization. They might be said to be purely "symbolic entities," but as such they are not thought of as *inherently* problematic.

This brings us back to the point made earlier, to which we can now add a supplementary point: the desexualization of ontology (that is, ontology no longer being conceived as a combinatory of two, "masculine" and "feminine" principles) coincides precisely with the sexual appearing as the real/disruptive point of being. This is why, if one "removes sex from sex," one removes the very thing that has brought to light the problem that sexual difference is all about. One does not remove the problem, but the means of seeing it, and of seeing the way it operates.

SEXUAL DIVISION, A PROBLEM IN ONTOLOGY

So far we have still been mostly discussing the question of sexuality in its peculiar ontological status. But how exactly does sexual *difference* enter this debate? What is the relationship between sexual difference and sexuality *tout court*? Is it accidental or essential? Which comes first? Is sexuality something that takes place because there is sexual difference? Freud's answer is unambiguous, and perhaps surprising: "The sexual drive is in the first instance independent of its object; nor is its origin likely to be due to its object's attractions" (Freud 1977a, 83). This is why, "from the point of view of psychoanalysis, the exclusive sexual interest felt by men for women is also a problem that needs elucidating and is not a self-evident fact based upon an attraction that is ultimately of a chemical nature" (ibid., 57). Moreover, he famously insists on the original nonexistence of any germ of two sexes (or two sexualities) during preadolescence. Let us start directly with this controversial passage:

> The auto-erotic activity of the erotogenic zones is, however, the same in both sexes, and owing to this uniformity there is no possibility of a distinction between the two sexes such as arises after puberty....Indeed, if we were able to give a more definite connotation to the concepts of "masculine" and "feminine," it would even be possible to maintain that libido is invariably and necessary of a masculine nature, whether it occurs in men or in women and irrespectively of whether its object is a man or a woman. (Freud 1977a, 141)

In other words, at the level of the libido there are not two sexes. And if we were able to say what exactly is "masculine" and "feminine," we would describe it as "masculine"—but we are precisely not able to say this, as Freud further emphasizes in the footnote attached to the quoted passage.[4]

So what exactly are we dealing with here, what is Freud saying in that passage? His formulations are especially interesting in relation to the spontaneous "liberal" understanding of sexual difference, pointing to a necessary ambivalence of sexual positions. According to this understanding, Masculinity and Femininity are just ideals (ideal genders) that exist nowhere in reality (no person is one hundred percent masculine or feminine); men and women exist only as differently portioned mixtures of these two ideal states (or "principles"—biological or otherwise). To put this in Nietzschean-sounding parlance: There are no Men and Women, only different degrees, different shades of masculinity and femininity....

What Freud is saying in the passage above, however, is something quite different from this "nobody is perfect" kind of wisdom; something much more interesting and counterintuitive. The point is not that if there were something like pure Masculinity and pure Femininity, we would be dealing with an ideal, clear case or model of sexual difference. Freud's point includes a much more paradoxical claim: if pure Masculinity and pure Femininity existed (if we were able to say what they are), they—or, rather, their sexuality—would be *one and the same* ("masculine"). But *since they do not exist, there is sexual difference*. In other words, sexual difference arises not from there being two sexes or two sexualities (at least in principle), but from the fact that there is no "second sex," and from an enigmatic *indifference* of the "sexual thing" (polymorphically perverse autoeroticism) that appears at the point of the "missing sex." Moreover, if the "second sex" is missing, this does not imply that we have only a "first sex" (masculinity), since one sex does not amount to "sex" at all: if there is only one sex, it is not a "sex" in any meaningful way....

To express it in a single formula: *What splits into two is the very nonexistence of the one* (that is, of the one which, if it existed, would be the Other).

Freud's paradoxical claims concerning sexuality and sexual difference receive a very elaborate conceptual treatment from Lacan, putting the question of sexuality and its split at the very core of psychoanalytic "ontology"—insofar as the latter includes the point of its own impossibility. Sexuality and sexual difference are absolutely, and irreducibly, linked to the signifying order, yet this does not mean that sexual difference is a symbolic construction. Sex is real because it marks an irreducible limit (contradiction) of the signifying order (and not something beyond or outside this order). There is, however, an important difference in conceiving this between Lacan's early and late work.

Lacan's early work is conceptually fortifying what he takes to be Freud's position, with the help of his theory of the signifying order and of his (or perhaps, rather, Kojève's) reading of Hegelian dialectics. His essay "The Signification of the Phallus" (1958) provides what is arguably the most concise formulation of this early position. The *presence* of the signifier induces an irredeemable loss on the part of the human animal: once it is articulated in the signifier (as "demand"), need is irreversibly alienated.

> Let us thus examine the effects of this presence [of the signifier]. They include, first, a deviation of man's needs due to the fact that he speaks: to the extent that his needs are subjected to demand, they come back to him in an alienated form.... What is thus alienated in needs constitutes an *Urverdrängung* [primal repression], as it cannot, hypothetically, be articulated in demand; it nevertheless appears in an offshoot that presents itself in man as desire (*das Begheren*). The phenomenology that emerges from analytic experience is certainly of a kind to demonstrate the paradoxical, deviant, erratic, eccentric, and even scandalous nature of desire that distinguishes it from need. (Lacan 2006c, 579)

This is indeed the basic outline of Lacan's early position: the presence of the signifier induces a "pure loss" on the—if I may put it this way—nonsignifying side of the human complex. This almost "physical" loss opens up the space of significations ("meaning effects") and of the dialectics of desire. And the phallus is famously defined by Lacan at this time as designating these "meaning effects as a whole" (ibid.).

Later on (notably at the beginning of the 1970s) Lacan all but reverses this perspective, by introducing (or rather by formalizing, since he had already introduced it earlier) a further complication of the signifying order itself: its being strictly coextensive with a signifying minus or lack. The "pure loss" now appears on the side of the signifier, which no longer has, or relates to, another side (pure organic need on which it would perform its inaugural operation); what it has is a reverse side (l'envers). Lacan has no hesitation in referring to this minus as the *foundation* (of the One of the signifying order).

In other words, it is no longer simply the presence of the signifier that induces the entire human "dialectics" and its contradictions, but rather an *absence* at the very heart of this presence, namely, a gap that appears together with the signifying order, as built into it. This rather shatters the self-evidence of the term "emergence of the signifier" to which we became accustomed in the Lacanian perspective: we have got used to speaking about nature being somehow interrupted, thrown out of joint, by the "emergence of the signifier." But what exactly does this mean? Does it mean the same thing as "the appearing of speech"? Especially in the context of Lacan's late work, it seems that we could also put things in a different "mythological" perspective—mythological to the extent that no narrative about the Beginning can avoid constructing a myth that best suits the real of actual observation. In this alternative perspective, the human (hi)story begins not with the emergence of the signifier, but with *one signifier "gone missing."* We could indeed say that nature is already full of signifiers (and at the same time indifferent to them); and that at some point one signifier "falls out," goes missing. And it is only from this that the "logic of the signifier" in the strict sense of the term is born (signifiers start to "run," and to relate to each other, across this gap). In this sense, and from this perspective, speech itself is already a response to the missing signifier, which *is not* (there). Speech is not simply "composed of signifiers," signifiers are not the (sufficient) condition of speech, the condition of speech as we know it is "one-signifier-less." Humans are beings roused from indifference and forced to speak (as well as to enjoy, since enjoyment appears at the place of this deficit) by one signifier gone missing. This temporal way of putting it ("gone missing") is an expression of what would be better formulated as the signifying structure emerging not simply without one signifier, but rather *with-without* one signifier—since this "hole" has consequences, and determines what gets structured around it.

Some time ago,[5] I tried to formulate this specific structure with the help of a joke which has often been used (by me and by others) since. I will nevertheless repeat it here, since it is difficult to find a better example to illustrate what is at stake:

A guy goes into a restaurant and says to the waiter: "Coffee without cream, please." The waiter replies: "I'm sorry, sir, but we're out of cream. Could it be without milk?"

The waiter's response introduces an additional, paradoxical spectral entity in the very dimension of negativity. The presupposition of his response is that "without" something actually means "with the lack of something," or with-without something. The signifying order appears with one signifier less in precisely this sense: not simply without one, but with-without one.

Two remarks could be added. First, it could well be that this late work by Lacan (who no longer refers to Hegel) is actually in many respects much closer to Hegel than his early work, where he refers to Hegel frequently.[6] And I would also say that this latter perspective, which seems much further from Freud and his elaborations of these issues, is in fact closer to Freud. In the "Three Essays on the Theory of Sexuality," Freud situates the operative cause of deviations from needs and instincts—the deviation constitutive of humankind—in the surplus excitation/satisfaction produced in the process of the satisfaction of somatic functions. "Oral pleasure," for example, which arises as a by-product of the satisfying of the need for food, starts to function as an autonomous object of the drive; it moves away from its first object and allows itself to be led into a series of substitute objects. All satisfaction of a need allows, in principle, for another satisfaction to occur, which tends to become independent and self-perpetuating in pursuing and reproducing itself. There is no natural need that could be absolutely pure, that is, devoid of this surplus element which splits it from within. That is to say: for Freud, the "human deviation" starts with a *surplus* (-enjoyment). In his early work, Lacan, skeptical of what seems to be Freud's attempt at explaining this deviation by a kind of linear causality starting from organic needs, replaces, as we have seen, the Freudian surplus with *loss*: deviation starts with "pure loss" induced by the signifier on the part of the body (as locus of the satisfaction of needs). Something of the need is irredeemably lost (cannot be articulated in a demand), and Lacan further links this to the concept/moment of primal repression. This originally lost bit of satisfaction then reappears within the signifying system (and among beings that populate it) as its transcendental condition: the absolute cause of desire. In his late work, Lacan, who situates the minus (or loss) on the side of the signifying order itself (which emerges with-without one signifier), actually comes closer to Freud, *provided* that we take into account the additional point on which I insisted earlier: that surplus-enjoyment itself is precisely what emerges at the place of the signifying deficit or hole. This topological addition (in respect to Freud) is what makes the Freudian observations quite compatible with Lacan's late work. That is to say: Lacan's step does not consist simply in complementing Freud's theory with the theory of the "emergence of the signifier"; rather, it consists in complementing it with the theory (or speculative hypothesis) of the lack of one signifier as the other side (*l'envers*) of the surplus-enjoyment which pertains to the satisfaction of all our needs. In order to understand this surplus-enjoyment (and its logic), we need to understand that it appears at the place of a signifying "hole" or minus. A further thing to point out is that this also affects the notion of primal repression (in Lacan): primal repression is now conceived as belonging to the signifying structure itself; it appears as "one with" the originally missing signifier, or as synonymous with the structure *with-without*.

And—here we come to the point which is most important for our discussion—sexual difference, or division, also originates in this ontological deficit. How to understand this? There are two predominant psychoanalytic conceptions of sexual difference. One reintroduces the duality of the sexes in the foundation itself (this would be the Jungian perspective of two complementary principles, yin–yang); the other starts with pure multiplicity as emphasized by Freud. According to this reading, what Freud analyzed as polymorphously perverse infantile sexuality shared by both boys and girls is a heterogeneous multiplicity which subsequently gets organized around two different positions by means of both hormonal and cultural "injections" and demands. Culture, which provides the normative framework and identification parameters of "masculinity" and "femininity," is said to be particularly determinant in this. One is usually careful to add that the original multiplicity and its contradictions are never fully resolved by our assuming of sexual positions, and the plurality of the sources of satisfaction are never fully absorbed in the genital sexual organization....

However, what results from Lacan's conceptualizations in his late work in relation to the question of sexual division is actually something else, which in a way reaffirms and conceptually fortifies the paradoxical formula implicit in Freud's remarks on the subject. As I put it earlier: *What splits into two is the very nonexistence of the one* (that is, of the one which, if it existed, would be the Other, the radically Other). What splits in two is the very "one that lacks," the minus, the with-without. This is how we could read Lacan's "formulas of sexuation": as two ways in which the constitutive minus of the signifying order is inscribed in this order itself, and dealt with. The operator which *marks* the constitutive minus of the symbolic order is written by Lacan as Φx (the "phallic function" or the "function of castration"—these are synonymous). In this sense we could say that castration is a subjectivizing reiteration of the inaugurating minus. And the next step brings us to the core of Lacan's revolutionary thinking of sexual difference: castration (or the "phallic function") is a universal function, a prerogative of subjectivity as such (regardless of sex), yet there is nothing sexually neutral about its operation; it always involves following the logic of this or that (sexed) position, and does not exist as a neutral foundation, or as a zero level of subjectivity. A "zero level" of subjectivity already involves a "decision," that is, this or that form of the "minus one." In other words, although the operator of castration is the prerogative of subjectivity, there is no subjectivity that would not handle it in this or that way, nor does "castration" exist outside the way in which it is handled. That is to say: there is no subjectivity beyond or beneath (or simply outside) the sexual division. Sexual difference is not a secondary distinction of subjectivity, or simply culturally constructed, since the means of the signifying construction of sexuality are already biased by the logical "parallax" by which the ontological deficit of the signifying order is inscribed in (or at work in) this same order. As Guy Le Gaufey insists with great persistence, Lacan's formulas of sexuation are not his attempt to "find a pertinent feature differentiating man and women" (Le Gaufey 2006, 86). Or, in another poignant formulation, "perhaps, the difference which keeps apart one [sex] from the other belongs neither to the one nor to the other" (ibid., 11). This was Joan Copjec's profound intuition when she discussed the formulas of sexuation in relation to the Kantian antinomies of reason: difference or contradiction does not so much exist *between* the two sides or positions. Rather, the two positions are parallel configurations of a difference or contradiction of the signifying order itself, which they logically decline in different ways (each one reproducing the fundamental contradiction in its own way).

What puts these two configurations in a (non-)relation is that they share the same function (Φx), yet at the same time this very fact prevents any kind of symmetry or complementarity between them. From a differentiating *feature* (based on the opposition presence/absence: some have it, some do not),[7] Lacan makes the phallus the signifier of the *difference as such*. What makes all the difference (for beings of speech) is "castration." The phallus does not constitute this difference, but signifies it, for both sexes (and regardless of whether one is homosexual or heterosexual). Sexual difference is a difference in configuring what makes all the difference: the minus marked by the phallic function as the function of castration. (The following diagram is reproduced from Lacan 2006c.)

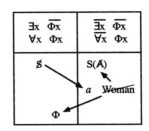

There are many extremely elaborate Lacanian readings of these formulas, providing and explaining their complex logical background, as well as interpreting their conceptual consequences.[8] It is not my purpose here to engage in a discussion of this sort and scope. I will confine myself to some remarks that could link these formulas to the specific ontological inquiry into the sexual which I am pursuing in this book.

The masculine (left) side posits that there exists One that is not castrated (and has access to full enjoyment: the primordial Father, the Woman):[9] $\exists x \overline{\Phi x}$. The *exclusion* of this One—that is, positing it as an exception, or exempting it—is the way in which the subject emerging on this side appropriates, frames, the minus involved in the signifying order. The exception (of a non-castrated One) functions as *constitutive*, that is, as the negative reference point, or the limit that permits everything else to be constituted as such, that is, to appear as *everything* else, or as a whole: all x are Φx, all x are subject to the function of castration ($\forall x\ \Phi x$). The exception is inscribed here in the very appearing of all *as all* (as a determined totality): this is how one has to read together the two formulas in the upper-left corner of the scheme. The logic at stake here is nicely summed up by the following joke: "There are no cannibals here, we ate the last one yesterday": the condition of "all of us" being "civilized" (non-cannibal) is the act of exemption that makes us "all." This is also what is at stake in the Freudian myth of the killing of the primordial Father (as possessor of all women), followed by *everyone* giving up the claim to an "unlimited enjoyment" represented by the figure of the primordial Father. The exception (the "killing") of the One frames the renunciation common to all. This basically means: everyone has to give up what they never had, and what is represented by the mythical figure of the primordial Father. The primordial Father is mythical in the precise sense that it is a necessary presupposition (and retrospective image) of the very notion of renunciation. Everyone has to give up what they never had—yet *the form of giving it up is nonetheless essential*. This is perhaps also the best definition of castration: to give up what one never had, that is to say, to transform the "minus one" which comes with the signifying order into something that we have renounced; to transform what we never had into something lost. In this kind of "framing" the negativity, the "negative quantity," of the signifier order acquires a signifying form, a privileged signifier; the lack of the signifier gets a signifier, and this signifier is called Phallus. This brings us to the lower part of the left side of the formulas of sexuation. What we see here is precisely that man assumes castration by relying on its *signifier* (Φ or the master-signifier, S_1—Lacan explicitly makes this connection) as the support of this subjective position, that is, as the support of "masculine" subjectivation.

This "assuming" it by means of the master-signifier—that is, by means of giving a signifying frame to the lack in the Other—equals assuming it by repressing it. One puts one's faith in the hands of the signifier, but one does not want to know anything about what takes place in this swap (namely, "castration"). The subject thus relies on the signifying support of castration, Φ (we can say: he doesn't need to know anything about castration because the signifier "knows" it for him),[10] and establishes a relation to the Other in the guise of the small a on the right-hand side of the formulas. What does this mean, or imply? The mythical One of exception (the One which, by being "cut out," so to speak, provides the signifying *frame* of the inaugural minus) also constitutes the frame or the "window of fantasy," as Lacan puts it, through which the other can appear as desirable (as object-cause of desire). In other words: the "formal" structure that provides the signifying frame for the lack of the signifier, combined with the particular circumstances in which this "swap" takes place for a subject, determines the concrete conditions under which (and only under which) the Other appears desirable. Hence Lacan's statement that man "never deals with anything by way of a partner but object a inscribed on the other side of the bar. He is unable to attain his sexual partner, who is the Other, except inasmuch as his partner is the cause of his desire" (Lacan 1999, 80). We have a nice illustration of this, to borrow one of Žižek's examples, in Hitchcock's movie *Rear Window*. James Stewart, immobilized by having his whole leg in plaster, is killing time by observing the people who live in the building opposite. A young nurse visits him every morning, and his fiancée (Grace Kelly) every evening. Grace Kelly is beautiful, rich, and crazy about Stewart. Yet he hardly seems to notice her, and is certainly in no hurry to marry her. Their relationship thus does not work too well, and they are on the verge of breaking it off. But this starts to change when they notice that strange things have been going on in one of the apartments across from Stewart's—it looks as if the man who lives there has just killed his wife. The young couple start playing detective together, and a decisive change in their relationship takes place when Kelly enters the apartment under investigation, appearing in the window. The supposed murderer is out, and she is looking for clues to the crime. Stewart is observing this from his own window: he watches her searching the apartment, and being surprised by the unexpected return of the man who lives there. This short sequence changes everything: Stewart behaves as if he were seeing Grace Kelly for the first time; she captures his full attention, and, completely fascinated, he can no longer take his eyes off her. Without a word being exchanged between them, we—as spectators—can see it all: now he very much desires her. She has quite literally entered the "window of his fantasy," and started to function as the object of his desire....

Let us now look on the other, feminine (right) side of the formulas of sexuation. Here the minus one that comes with the signifying order (constituting its real) configures differently: castration, as the signifying operator of the minus, does not rely for the feminine subject on the exclusion (exception) of the non-castrated Other. We start with negation of a possible exception, $\overline{\exists x}\ \overline{\Phi x}$: there is no x which does not fall under the phallic function (that is, under the function of castration). Castration allows for no exception. And it is precisely this that makes any universal statement impossible, as we read in the second line of the "feminine" formulas: not all x are Φx. We cannot speak of "all" women or, simply, of the woman. Why is the possibility of an exception excluded on this, the feminine side? What does it mean or imply? It is the logical writing of the juncture of the following two claims. First, woman is "the Other, in the most radical sense, in the sexual relationship" (Lacan 1999, 81). And second, "there is no Other of the Other." If woman is the Other of man, man is not the Other of woman. There is no Other of the Other—the Other is included in the Other (as the Other sex). This is what is expressed by the following paradoxical formulation: "Being the Other..., woman is that which has a relationship to that Other" (ibid.). In other words, the relationship to the Other is, so to speak, included in the Other; it is "part" of the Other. Whereas a man can think of the Other as the exception to the rule, to his rule, on the basis of which he relates to women, a woman cannot think of the Other as the exception to her rule, but as part of the rule, as included in the rule. This affects significantly the nature of this rule, making it "not-all." The nonexistence of the Other is itself inscribed into the Other. And this is precisely what the concept of the unconscious is about: the point where the nonexistence of the Other is itself inscribed into the Other. And, as suggested by the concept of the unconscious, this is not a point of self-reflective transparency, but that of a signifying *gap* constitutive of knowledge. This further implies that the infamous Lacanian "barred Other" is not simply an inconsistent, lacking Other, but the Other the inconsistency of which is inscribed in it, and has itself a marker in it: Lacan writes it as S(Ⱥ), signifier of the Other as barred. But what is this signifier? Here Lacan makes a most surprising connection: "by S(Ⱥ) I designate nothing other than woman's *jouissance*" (Lacan 1999, 84). The signifier at stake is thus a most peculiar one. In order to understand what precisely is at stake here, we can relate it directly to the following crucial claim, made above: the emergence of the signifying order directly coincides with the non-emergence of one signifier, and *at the place of this gap appears enjoyment* as the heterogeneous element pertaining to the signifying structure, yet irreducible to it. In this precise sense, the enjoyment at stake essentially belongs to the unconscious (and to its "gap"): not as repressed, but as the very substance of the missing signifier which, as missing, gives its form to the unconscious. This also explains Lacan's emphasis (in *Seminar XX*, where he discusses formulas of sexuation) on the question of knowledge and its "limits": Can one know—and say—anything about this other, non-phallic enjoyment? The answer is no: one cannot say anything about this enjoyment, this other enjoyment cannot be an object of knowledge, because it is a place-holder for the knowledge which does not exist. This enjoyment appears at the place of the lack in knowledge, it appears *because there is nothing to know there*. In this precise sense, woman's *jouissance* is the signifier of the lack of knowledge (in the Other). It marks the point where the Other does not know. If there was such a thing as "sexual relation," this would amount to the existence of its signifier (knowledge) in the Other, but since there is no sexual relation, there is this other enjoyment. What this implies is that the infamous "feminine *jouissance*" is not an obstacle to the sexual relation, but a symptom (or marker) of its nonexistence. No wonder, then, that it has been subjected to such violent forms of exorcism in the course of history.

This $S(\not{A})$, the other's *jouissance* as the signifier of the "Other as barred," is thus not to be confused with the signifier of castration (Φ, or the phallic function), with which a woman also has a relation: "woman has a relation-ship with $S(\not{A})$, and it is already in that respect that she is doubled, that she is not-whole, since she can also have a relation with Φ" (Lacan 1999, 81). The relation with Φ—that is to say, the relation with the signifier—is the relation on which existence is founded (for any speaking being), whereas the rela-tion with $S(\not{A})$ puts us on the path of "ex-sistence." But the point is not sim-ply that a woman only partly falls under the phallic function, that she is not "whole" in it, and that part of her remains outside. No, "she is there in full" (ibid., 74). But there is something else (*en plus*), which comes with the posi-tion of being the Other in the sexual relation, and this *supplement*—the rela-tion with $S(\not{A})$—not only detotalizes her, but also makes her relation with Φ different than in the case of a man.

We could perhaps put it in the following way: Being the Other in the sexual relationship, a woman cannot rely (for her being) on a constitutive *exception*, but relies on a constitutive *deception*. This, at least, was the remark-able idea suggested by Joan Riviere in her essay "Womanliness as Masquer-ade," where she suggests that femininity is essentially a masquerade, a putting on of femininity. Needless to say, this point was much appreciated by Lacan. Riviere proceeds in two steps. She starts from a case study of a woman who was extremely successful in what was then considered an intellectual "male" profession (involving public speaking and writing), who, particularly after a successful public performance, tended to react with an excessive display of femininity, by compulsive flirting and coquetry. What analysis revealed in this particular case, and in Riviere's account, was the following:

> [Her compulsive ogling and coquetting] was an unconscious attempt to ward off the anxiety which would ensue on account of the reprisals she anticipated from the father-figures after her intellectual performance. The exhibition in public of her intellectual proficiency, which was in itself

carried through successfully, signified an exhibition of herself in possession of the father's penis, having castrated him. The display once over, she was seized by horrible dread of the retribution the father would then exact. (Riviere 1929, 305)

To ward off this anxiety she engaged in coquetting and a display of femininity, "'disguising herself' as merely a castrated woman, [so that] in that guise the man found no stolen property on her" (ibid., 306). This is not to say, of course, that while she was "disguising herself" as castrated, in truth she was not. Behind her disguise there was not something like a full non-castrated subjectivity, but a full-blown anxiety, on which I will comment later.

It is only fair to say that Riviere's account of the case in question often reads as an oversimplified application of psychoanalytic theory and its "ready-made" concepts, rather than as analysis proper. Yet crucial for our argument here is her next step, which brought the article its (deserved) fame, and in which she arrives at a more general conclusion, not necessarily related to this particular woman's history and psyche: femininity (or womanliness) as such is nothing but this susceptibility to wear femininity as a mask (that is to say, to wear castration as a mask). There is no "true femininity" as opposed to femininity as masquerade:

> The reader may now ask how I define womanliness or where I draw the line between genuine womanliness and the "masquerade." My suggestion is not, however, that there is any such difference; whether radical or superficial. They are the same thing. (Riviere 1929, 306)

One can be a woman only if one is not "intrinsically so"—at its most genuine, femininity is masquerade. In this precise sense it is perhaps not enough to say that there is no essence of femininity; one could go a step further and say that the essence of femininity is to pretend to be a woman.

One is a woman if one carries castration as a mask. Castration is not repressed (or it is repressed, but to a lesser extent than in the case of men), neither is it assumed as something empirical. That emphasis is crucial, since this is not about revealing, disclosing, or "accepting" any kind of empirical fact—for example, that "she doesn't have it"; it is not that she openly reveals that she is "castrated": castration can only be enacted, the real of castration is not something that could be exposed or seen as such. Nobody has it (namely, the missing signifier), men no more so than women; what they both have is a way of dealing with this ontological minus by dealing with its marker (phallic function as the function of castration). And if using it as a mask defines the feminine position, this does not prevent men from using it as a mask as well: this is why an ostentatious display of virility (men meticulously dressing up in "masculine" clothes or, for example, in costumes of symbolic power) always has the curious effect of seeming feminine. The "phallic function" is not masculine: what we perceive as "masculinity" and "femininity" are different ways of its deployment. "Putting it on" suggests femininity. But "putting it on *what?*"

This question leads us back to the anxiety that Riviere emphasizes in her analysis and which, I will suggest, goes beyond the fear of reprisals (by father figures) which she underlines, and joins what could be seen as a more general "feminine anxiety": anxiety pertaining to femininity as essentially a masquerade. This path is implicitly indicated by Riviere herself: she keeps repeating the same metaphor in her description of the dread that compels the woman from her analysis to "disguise herself as castrated" after every (public) achievement: the metaphor of "stolen goods" or "stolen property." Her display of femininity, writes Riviere, was "much as a thief will turn out his pockets and ask to be searched to prove that he does not have the stolen goods." What I would add to Riviere's analysis at this point is simply the following: at stake here is not simply the dread of being punished for stealing the father's property, but also, and more fundamentally, the anxiety of literally *being nothing*: if her intellectual performance was attributable to stolen property, then who, or what, or where, is "she"? In other words, the really troubling question here is: What if I'm not really anything, what if there is no "me" in any of this? This ontological anxiety doesn't stop at "Am I that name?," rather, it revolves around "Do I exist at all?" All that I have left at this point is a pretense, a mask. The subject hinges on this mask, and not perhaps the other way around. Under the mask there is nothing but sheer ontological anxiety.

According to Lacan, this radical ontological anxiety is the *prerogative of subjectivity as such*; and precisely in this sense, the feminine position is the closest to subjectivity in its pure state. To be a man implies a step in a different direction—relying on the phallus as his signifying support (as "that which props him up," as Lacan puts it)—he *believes* that he *is* (exists), which is why "male anxiety" usually stops at castration anxiety. Man is the subject who believes he is man. Masculinity is a question of belief (based on, and sustained by, the repression of castration).

Of course, believing oneself to be a man does not exclude the painful anxiety about how much of a man one is; on the contrary: only those who fundamentally believe themselves to be men can have this kind of worry, or anxiety.... This, by the way, also sheds some light on why it often happens that apropos of women who excel in "male" professions, one asks whether they are "really women." To conclude that they are not really women but "men" ("mannish" or homosexual) seems to result in relief—relief from what? From the anxiety (dread) that behind these accomplishments there is no substantial subjectivity and that, furthermore, this could be a *general state of things*, with masculinity being but a simulacrum of a substantial subjectivity. When men feel threatened by such women, it is not simply that they represent for them a "threat of castration"; rather, their presence makes it harder for men to sustain the repression of castration; it weakens the defense wall of anxiety. And this explains the often violent and affect-ridden reactions to these women.

So this, then, is how sexual division could be formulated from the perspective of the question of the ontological minus: masculinity is a matter of *belief*, femininity is a matter of *pretense*. And one can (it is to be hoped) see from this formulation in what sense the psychoanalytic take on sexual difference is not about finding a pertinent *feature* differentiating men and women; it is about the parallax inscription of the constitutive minus of the signifying order *in this order itself*. This could well be why Lacan never actually uses the term sexual difference, but speaks of sexual "division." This is also why, for him, language is not a neutral medium of communication between subjects, but produces subjects by implicating them in its inherent antagonism, its own inherent contradiction and impossibility. Subjects are not "constructed" by language; they are produced as a response to its inherent limit, and the unexpected plus appearing at this limit.

Although it is formulated more explicitly much later, this fundamental insight is already implicit in the perspective from which Lacan, in his 1957 essay "The Instance of the Letter in the Unconscious," criticizes the logic usually associated with structural linguistics, and particularly with the famous Saussurean algorithm (S/s—signifier over signified). The central theme of structural linguistics is the emphasis on pure differentiality (as Saussure famously puts it in his *Course in General Linguistics*: in language there are only differences without positive terms, and signifiers "make sense," or produce meaning, only as parts of differential networks of places, binary oppositions, etc.), as well as the emphasis on the arbitrariness of the sign: the signifying chain is strictly *separated* from the signified, which is what the bar in the Saussurean algorithm indicates. This algorithm, argues Lacan, can sustain the illusion that the signifier serves the function of representing the signified, and that it has to justify its existence in terms of some signification. To illustrate this erroneous conception, Lacan first reproduces what he calls "the faulty illustration" (reproduced from Lacan 2006c):

TREE

The signifier "tree" would serve (albeit arbitrarily) to represent some signification. This is the conception that Lacan refutes as erroneous. On the other hand, he is also well aware that it is not enough to simply assert that there is no connection whatsoever between the two levels of the algorithm, and to subtract from the algorithm S/s solely the notion of the parallelism of its upper and lower terms, because this way "it remains the enigmatic sign of a total mystery. Which, of course, is not the case" (Lacan 2007, 416).

For Lacan there is a connection between the two levels, but it is not that of representation, nor that of signification. So, what is it? How to think it without falling back into the (pre-Saussurean) position of seeing language as a collection of names for a collection of objects? Lacan's answer is that "the signifier in fact enters the signified—namely, in a form which, since it is not immaterial, raises the question of its place in reality" (Lacan 2007, 417). This, then, is the connection we were looking for: the signifier "enters the signified," and the bar between them does not exactly prevent that. But how can we understand this? I believe it is quite legitimate to understand the singular connection at stake in terms of "*with-without*" as discussed above. The signifier does not represent a signified, nor is it simply "an enigmatic sign of a total mystery"—it is *with-without the signified* (as the binary signifier). The lack of the relation symbolized by the bar between the two levels is itself *inherent to* the signifier (and the signifying order) as such. It should not be conceived simply as the incapacity of the signifier to find, attain (and relate to) its signified, but rather as language's *inherent* minus and contradiction. This is the inherent twirl/loop of the symbolic order, the (same) minus implied and repeated by every word we utter. What links/relates one signifier to another (constituting the signifying chain) is precisely the negativity of with-without: this is the gap inherent to the signifying order where Lacan situates the *subject* (of the unconscious). And the beauty of it is, of course, that this with-without is already there in the signifier without: with-out—to be without something is to be with the lack of something. We could thus say that Lacan transposed the bar separating the signifier from the signified (S/s) into the bar inherent to the register of the signifier itself. "A signifier represents the subject for another signifier" is his formula that makes this binding negativity explicit. And this is also why, for Lacan, the theory of the signifier is inseparable from the theory of the unconscious—the "with-without" (or simply with-out) could also be taken as the very formula (the letter) of the unconscious; not of any unconscious content, but of the very form (topology, structure) of the unconscious. The signifier and the unconscious (or the subject of the unconscious) are inseparable concepts; the signifying order (emerging with-without one signifier) and the constitution (of the loop) of the unconscious are one and the same thing.

For Saussure, language functions as a system of pure differentiality. Meaning emerges through relations of difference that a signifier maintains in relation to other signifiers ("tree" is tree because it is not "car," "bush," "train," and so on). In language, everything is thus based on relations. Lacan's point, however, which moves beyond Saussure and the classical structuralist approach, is that this pure relational differentiality, which he admits, can only be based on a non-relation or, if one prefers, on a *different kind of difference*. In order for the relational differentiality to exist and to function, the *one* (of the binary relation) has to be missing. And this makes all the difference (the possibility of differentiation can appear only on the basis of this fundamental difference). This is Lacan's crucial addition which allows him to reintroduce the concept of the subject (of the unconscious) at the very highest point of the structuralist attacking of this notion.

And, as I have been arguing so far, the real of sexual division is linked to precisely this point of the "missing one." I would further suggest that this is why Lacan uses as a key example of his general understanding of the functioning of the signifier the following, also quite famous, drawing (reproduced from Lacan 1999):

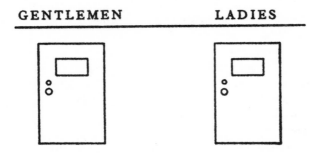

GENTLEMEN   LADIES

This is the drawing (illustration) with which he replaces the "faulty illustration" (the one involving the tree). What do we have here? Two different names written above (the repetition of) the same thing, a door. In other words, we have differentiality (two different signifiers), but there is nothing different in the realities to which they refer. And yet they are not one reality, but reality as split. Lacan is quick to add that his point is not merely to silence the nominalist debate with a low blow, "but to show how the signifier in fact enters the signified" (Lacan 2007, 417).

There is nothing neutral in this example; on the contrary, it is highly biased. For it cannot be taken and understood outside Lacan's persistent emphasis on how sexual difference is a singular kind of difference, which does not follow the basic signifying logic of binary oppositions and differentiations.[11] We thus seem to be facing an obvious contradiction: how can Lacan use, as his showcase illustration of the functioning of the signifier, an example that, according to his own theory, does not fall under the usual rules of functioning of the signifier? The answer is that what Lacan is after here—in his debate with structural linguistics—is not simply an example of the functioning of the signifier, but also an example of the *presuppositions* of this functioning: presuppositions left out by linguistics, and brought into focus by psychoanalysis.

In other words, the "Ladies and Gentlemen" example is not so much an example of the logic of the signifier as the example "illustrating" the constitutive gap and contradiction at the very core of the signifying logic; it is not one of many possible examples, but rather an example which, in a sense, is implicit in any other example decomposed to the level of its presuppositions. The example used by Lacan at this crucial point of his theory of the signifier is thus by no means accidental, which becomes abundantly clear when he goes on to replace this "contrived example," as he calls it (the above schema), with a "lived experience of truth," namely, the following story:

A train arrives at a station. A little boy and a little girl, brother and sister, are seated across from each other in a compartment next to the outside window that provides a view of the station platform buildings going by as the train comes to a stop. "Look," says the brother, "we're at Ladies!" "Imbecile!" replies his sister, "don't you see we're at Gentlemen."

And he accompanies this story with a very precise, and beautiful, commentary:

> one would have to be half-blind to be confused as to the respective places of the signifier and the signified here, and not to follow from what radiant center the signifier reflects its light into the darkness of incomplete significations.
>
> For the signifier will raise Dissension that is merely animal in kind, and destined to the natural fog of forgetfulness, to the immeasurable power of ideological warfare, which is merciless to families and a torment to the gods. To these children, Gentlemen and Ladies will henceforth be two homelands toward which each of their souls will take flight on divergent wings, and regarding which it will be all the more impossible for them to reach an agreement since, being in fact the same homeland, neither can give ground regarding the one's unsurpassed excellence without detracting from the other's glory. (Lacan 2007, 417)

This passage is extremely valuable because we can clearly see how, for Lacan, two topics (the topic of the logic of the signifier and the topic of sexual division) coincide; he treats them as inseparable. Not because the signifier would already presuppose sexual difference, or construct it as such, but because sexual difference (and all the contrived dialectics of sexuality, desire, love) is the consequence—not simply of the signifying order, but of *the fact that something is lacking in it* (and that, at the same time, there is something excessive in it—surplus-enjoyment). As two perspectives *within* the same signifying configuration, the (not quite) two sexualized subjects mark a radical difference, or difference as such. This is the difference that has no ground: it does not spring from two different grounds, which would allow it to settle as difference between two "homelands" (which could then sign an agreement, and establish a "relation"). Their homeland is one and the same: yet this oneness and sameness is the oneness and sameness of pure difference.[12]

Lacan's example is thus not simply an example of the functioning of the signifier, but also and above all an example of its negative ontological presuppositions; it is an example of what pins the dimension of language to the gap of the unconscious, to a "radical heteronomy...gaping within man" (Lacan 2007, 436), as he puts it. This heteronomy is thus not that between Ladies and Gentlemen, but between language as a system of differences and the object-like surplus (*a*) appearing at the place of the constitutive minus of this system, spoiling its pure differentiality. Sexual difference is difference in the configuration (logic) of this "spoiling." This is the other point where psychoanalysis parts from structural linguistics. If we consider the phenomena of speech that psychoanalysis mostly deals with, it is simply not true that all meaning is produced according to the laws of pure differentiality, but also following two other mechanisms pointed out by Freud: sonorous similarities or homonyms, and associations that exist in the speaker's memory. Slips of the tongue, jokes, dreams—in all these (and others) we find something very much like positive entities, with words functioning in a strangely similar fashion to objects. Lacan thought this Freudian point was crucial.[13]

Signifiers are never pure signifiers. They are ridden, from within, with unexpected surpluses that tend to ruin the logic of their pure differentiality. On the one side—the structuralist side that Lacan includes in his theory—they are separated from the signified in the sense that there is no inherent connection leading from the signifier to its meaning. Yet, if this were all, the signifying field would be a consistent system and, as the structuralist motto goes, a structure without a subject. Lacan subscribes to this view to the extent to which it convincingly does away with the notion of a "psychological subject," of an intentional subjectivity using language for its purposes, mastering the field of speech or being its Cause and Source. Yet he goes a step further. If we focus on the signifying chain, precisely in its independence and autonomy, we are bound to notice that it constantly produces, from within itself, quite unexpected effects of meaning, a meaning which is, strictly speaking, a surplus meaning that stains the signifiers from within. This is the locus of the subject (of the unconscious). And it is precisely through this surplus meaning (bound up with surplus-enjoyment) that signifiers are irreducibly and intrinsically bound to the reality to which they refer; it is in this way that they "enter the signified." We can thus supplement our thesis according to which this "entering the signified" could be understood in terms of with-without which marks an absence at the very heart of the signifying presence: supplement it by this dimension or element of surplus meaning/enjoyment as the other side (l'envers) of the negativity implied in the with-without. The signifier enters the signified (in a form "which is not immaterial," as Lacan adds), and thus takes a place in reality, in the form of this surplus which creates, as well as complicates, the signifying relations, twisting and "driving" their logic.

Minus one/plus enjoyment—this is the necessarily distorted structural topology where the subject of the unconscious dwells. This subject is never neuter; it is sexed, since sex(uality) is nothing but a configuring of the signifying minus and of the surplus-enjoyment: a configuring which cannot escape contradiction, the latter being the *logical* consequence of the one (the Other) that is not there.

JE TE M'ATHÈME ... MOI NON PLUS

Alain Badiou and Barbara Cassin have a long history of an intriguing dissent regarding the role of sophistry in philosophy. To put it very simply: Badiou sees in the figure of the sophist the antiphilosopher *par excellence*, tempting the philosopher to discard the notion and pursuit of truth, and instead to embrace a playful gliding on the surface of language and sense, exposing and enjoying its contradictions and paradoxes. In other words, the sophist is the fatal double, the *alter ego* of a true philosopher; he is the Other which philosophy—even though it can indeed learn something from him—has to leave behind in the end. On the other hand, Barbara Cassin, who has written most compellingly on sophistry and the figure of the sophist,[14] sees in this figure an irreducible and indispensable core of philosophy: something that one cannot eliminate from philosophy without losing philosophy itself. Sophistry is a genuine philosophy.

And it is surely no coincidence that this polemic reaches its peak and crystallizes precisely around (the late work of) Lacan, in which we find proliferating side by side, and at the same time, the taste for "sophistry" (plays on words, equivocation, neologisms...) and formal rigorism (formulas, mathemes, topology). In 2010, Badiou and Cassin published a short book entitled *Il n'y a pas de rapport sexuel*, which features their respective commentaries on Lacan's notoriously difficult text from 1972, "L'étourdit." It is quite obvious that the title ("There is no sexual relation") has not been chosen simply because they both discuss what is at stake in this Lacanian claim, and in his formulas of sexuation, but also because they believe that their discussion is itself a staging of this claim, its philosophical and embodied performance. In the introduction to the book, signed by both, we read:

These two studies, or readings, or ruptures, made by a woman and a man (this remark is important), turn around knowledge, contemplated by her from the perspective of its intimate relation to the matters of language, and by him from the perspective of what philosophy pretends to be able to say concerning the truth. And this is why in relation to Lacan's "L'étourdit," to the modern theory of sexuation, to the paradoxes of language and of the unconscious, the philosopher at least finds it possible to say that what follows is a new confrontation, or a new dividing up [*partage*], between the masculinity of Plato and the femininity of sophistry. (Badiou and Cassin 2010, 9)

Hm...

Upon reading the two essays, we are indeed immediately struck by the divergence in the fundamental perspective and conceptual wager of the two authors. Barbara Cassin puts at the center of her reading Lacan's emphasis on *equivocity*, formulated most directly in the following claim from "L'étourdit": "The interpretation which—if it is not to be directive, has to be ambiguous or equivocal—is here in order to bore a hole" (Lacan 1973, 48). Or, to quote a slightly more extensive version of the same claim:

Psychoanalytic intervention should in no way be theoretical, suggestive, that is to say imperative. It has to be *equivocal*. Analytical interpretation is not made in order for it to be understood; it is made in order to make waves... (Lacan 1976, 32)

Badiou, on the other hand, takes for his starting point another well-known claim by Lacan: "formalization is our goal, our ideal" (Lacan 1999, 119). Here, the emphasis is strikingly different: we are in the domain of formalization, formulas, mathemes, knots, and other topological models, and all this (including the clinical practice of *la passe*) is based upon the idea of an integral transmission, a transmission without any rest. What this implies, according to Badiou, is an absolute *univocity*. At the level of the matheme there is no equivocity—the matheme is only what it is.

Many years ago, when Badiou first presented his theory of love, in which he made ample use of mathematical formalization, a journalist thought his approach was terribly reductive in relation to the rich lived experience of love. In an attempt to mock Badiou, he came up with a splendid formula, very much appreciated by Badiou. He said that when Badiou is making love to a woman, he probably doesn't say to her: *Je t'aime* but, rather: *Je te m'athème*.[15] And perhaps an interesting way of summarizing the debate between Badiou and Cassin on these questions of equivocity versus formalization, cast in terms of sexual difference, would be to paraphrase the famous song, and to say that this is their *Je te m'athème... moi non plus*.

Yet is this view on sexual difference—as the divide "between the masculinity of Plato and the femininity of sophistry," or between univocity and equivocity—really sustainable from a Lacanian perspective?

Needless to say, both Cassin's and Badiou's readings are based on the appropriate passages from Lacan, and it might seem that they testify in this way to the inconsistency of Lacan's thought, or at least to his being clearly divided between two opposite tendencies: the almost wordless mode of formalization, and the abundantly talkative mode of puns, playing with words, as well as of the labyrinthine path of mysterious- sounding formulations. It is true: in Lacan we find both.

Yet this opposition or difference between equivocity and formalization (univocity) in the context of Lacan's theory may actually be misleading, or simply false. It is based on the opposition and divergence between two philosophical orientations, defined by Badiou in terms of the pursuit of truth (and formalization) *versus* the "linguistic turn." Yet it is crucial to see how the very notion of *language* that follows from psychoanalytic theory and practice is not the one implied in the "linguistic turn," and does not allow for this kind of opposition, but rather makes it unsustainable. This at least is what I will be arguing in what follows, taking Badiou's and Cassin's commentaries on Lacan's text only as a starting point, without presenting and doing justice to their complex, and in many ways most illuminating, arguments. The question that will guide us is simply this: how are equivocity and formalization configured in Lacan, and what is the position of truth in this configuration?

Let us first briefly return to the quotes where Lacan rejects the imperative nature of interpretation in favor of equivocity. Psychoanalytic intervention and interpretation should not be "theoretical," "suggestive," "directive," "imperative"—what does this mean in fact? It is important first to stress that what is at stake here is not some kind of antitheoretical orientation of psychoanalysis, as analysts sometimes like to understand from such claims—what Lacan critiques here is not psychoanalytic theory, but the kind of *practice* which brings theory into play at the wrong point or in the wrong way. Let us hear the words from Lacan himself, who this time spells out very clearly what is at stake:

> If there is a principal law of psychoanalysis, it is that we shouldn't blather, not even in the name of analytical categories. No wild analysis: one shouldn't be using words that make sense only for the analyst. I learn everything from my analysands; it is from them that I learn what psychoanalysis is about. I borrow my interventions from them, and not from my teaching—except if I know that they know exactly what something means. I replaced the word "word" by the word "signifier"; and this means that it lends itself to equivocity, to several possible meanings. And if you choose your words well— the words that will haunt the analysand—you will find the elected signifier, the one which will work. (Lacan 1976, 34)

It is not out of (false or sincere) modesty that Lacan says "I learn everything from my analysands," "I borrow my interventions from them." Rather, this is a procedure, a method that is carefully thought out, and actually recalls Hegel's warning, in the Preface to the *Phenomenology of Spirit*, against the kind of (philosophical) proceeding which concerns itself only with aims and results, with differentiating and passing judgments on things. This kind of activity, says Hegel, instead of getting involved with the thing, is always-already beyond it; instead of tarrying with it, and being preoccupied with it, this kind of knowing remains essentially preoccupied with itself (Hegel 1977, 3). The proximity of "practicing analyst" Lacan and "speculative philosopher" Hegel on these questions of method should be enough to prevent any hasty conclusions drawn in terms of theory versus practice, philosophy versus antiphilosophy, or singular versus universal.

A psychoanalyst is not an expert treating patients with her expertise, which she would apply to symptoms of a given concrete case. If one wants to shift something in the thing (in the unconscious structure), one has to allow it to speak, for it alone can come up with, produce, the *word that eventually "works,"* moves things. But one—in this case the analyst—should of course be able to recognize the "right word." And this is not simply a practical (clinical) stance, but also a theoretical one.

To return to our central question: what does this emphasis on the equivocal imply in relation to the also clearly stated ideal of formalization, which is very much present in Lacan's work?

The answer may be surprising in its very simplicity: equivocity itself can function *directly* as a formula, as is clear already in the example of "*Je te m'athème*," as well as, for instance, in how equivocal punch lines function in jokes. In the case of jokes, playing on equivocity, and introducing another meaning with its help, does not have the result of relativizing meaning; it is, rather, designed so that we get a very precise, isolated point. Let me repeat here a joke that I used in my book on comedy. It is worth repeating not only because it illustrates this point perfectly, but also because we will be able to reconfigure it and use it further on as an example of possible analytic intervention.

A man comes home from an exhausting day at work, plops down on the couch in front of the television, and tells his wife: "Get me a beer before it starts."

The wife sighs and gets him a beer. Fifteen minutes later, he says: "Get me another beer before it starts." She looks cross, but fetches another beer and slams it down next to him. He finishes that beer and a few minutes later says: "Quick, get me another beer, it's going to start any minute." The wife is furious.

She yells at him: "Is that all you're going to do tonight? Drink beer and sit in front of that TV? You're nothing but a lazy, drunken, fat slob, and furthermore..."

The man sighs, and says: "It's started..."

The final punch line is equivocal, yet the point it transmits is not. This kind of equivocal punch line does not open up a multiplicity of possible meanings; rather, it evokes and uses this multiplicity in order to efficiently pin down and transmit a *singular point* (or impasse); and to transmit it in a most economical way—not by fully and exhaustively describing it, but by directly naming it: that is, precisely, so that it functions somewhat like a formula. It is of course true that such "formulas" are "universally transmittable" only if one speaks the language "of which" they are made. Unlike mathematical formulas they depend on living languages, on people speaking them. But this is not so much a limitation as precisely that which makes it possible for these equivocities to work as formulas, and to work *tout court*: to "make waves," to "bore a hole"—to have consequences for the reality which they formalize.

What is a symptom that one "brings" to analysis? It is always a subjective *solution* to some contradiction or impasse. And it is a solution that usually makes one's life very complicated; it comes with some degree of suffering. Yet it is a solution, and it involves serious subjective investment. The work of analysis consists in forcing out the contradiction "solved" by the symptom, in relating the symptom to the singular contradiction of which it is a solution. Psychoanalysis does not solve the contradiction; rather, it solves its solution (given by the symptom). It *bores a hole* where the symptom has built a dense net of significations. And the subject needs to "reconstruct" herself as part of this contradiction, as directly implied in it. (To be sure, this does not mean that here we are on the level of the particular/individual, as opposed to the general or communal. The contradiction that affects an individual is *intrinsically* social—others, and our relation to them, as well as social relations more generally, are already implied in it.)

The right (equivocal) word "bores a hole" because it repeats/names the enjoyment that holds ("glues") different meanings together in a symptomatic way. It brings out the negativity (contradiction) which is shared, repeated, and obfuscated by the deployment of these different meanings, and it does so by spoiling/dissolving the enjoyment (surplus excitation) that emerges at the place of this negativity or contradiction (and associates these different meanings). The right word is not the right word by virtue of what it means, but by virtue of what it accomplishes.

What is at stake here is thus perhaps not best staged in terms of the relationship (or opposition) between equivocity and univocity. As Lacan himself suggests, univocity is, rather, a characteristic of the symbols of animal language.

> All that appears-is (*parest*) in [language] of a *semblant* of communication is always dream, lapsus, or joke. Nothing to do then with what is imagined or confirmed in many points of animal language. The real there is not to be distanced from a univocal communication, from which the animals as well, in giving us the model, would make us their dolphins: a function of code exercises itself in it....Even more, some vital conducts organize themselves there with symbols in every respect similar to ours (erection of an object to the rank of a master-signifier in the order of the flight of migration, symbolism of the parade as often amorous as of combat, signals of labor, marks of territory), except that these symbols are never equivocal. (Lacan 1973, 47)

Equivocity, on the other hand, is the very inherent condition of formalization, insofar as the formalization is not to be confused with symbols and codes as they seem to function between animals. In psychoanalysis, formalization is not a formalization of this or that content, of this or that meaning (as "the right meaning")—it is the formalization of the very impasse/"hole" through which (and only through which) these meanings exist as bound together in a given configuration. Free associations produce piles of associated meanings. And the right word is the key to the twisted logic of this association. How do we know we have the right key? Because it works—it works in the direction of *disassociation*. The key in psychoanalysis is not simply a hermeneutical key, although hermeneutics is also important.

As Slavoj Žižek formulated this in relation to the Freudian theory of dreams and to his thesis that "dreams are nothing other than a particular form of thinking" (Freud 1988, 650):

> First we must break the appearance according to which a dream is nothing but a simple and meaningless confusion, a disorder caused by physiological processes and as such having nothing whatsoever to do with signification. In other words, we must accomplish a crucial step towards a *hermeneutical* approach and conceive the dream as a meaningful phenomenon, as something transmitting a repressed message which has to be discovered by an interpretative procedure.
>
> Then we must get rid of the fascination in this kernel of signification, in the "hidden meaning" of the dream—that is to say, in the content concealed behind the form of a dream—and center our attention on this form itself, on the dream-work to which the "latent dream-thoughts" were submitted. (Žižek 1989, 14)

The unconscious desire is not the content of the hidden message, it is the active designer of the form that latent thoughts get in a dream.

This is why the key in psychoanalysis is not a key to a hidden meaning, but the key that "*unlocks*" this form itself (makes what has been associated to compose the hidden meaning dissociate). And this is what "the right word" does.

We could actually reconfigure the "It's started..." joke as something that constitutes a possible psychoanalytic intervention. A patient is repeatedly complaining to his analyst how, when he comes home from work, all he wants is to lie on the couch, drink beer, and watch his favorite TV show. He insists, repeatedly, on how much he likes to have a few beers before the show starts, which is why he has the habit of asking his wife just this: to bring him a beer or two *before it starts*. Yet inevitably, he complains, his wife explodes and starts shouting insults at him.—"*And so it starts*," intervenes the analyst. The point of this intervention is not simply that the true hidden meaning behind the husband's repeating of the words "before it starts" is a reference to frequent domestic quarrels, but also to shift the focus to the form itself: this whole staging (the whole scene as acted out with his wife) IS *his favorite show*. And this point is made not simply so that the husband will understand what he is really saying, but also to spoil for him the symptomatic enjoyment invested in this scene of the domestic quarrel and its anticipation. In this precise sense we could say that the form of the symptom (the specific work of the unconscious) is "unlocked" by this intervention.

The psychoanalytic key could thus be described precisely as fitting the point where "truth holds onto the real," to use Lacan's wording from *Television*: "I always speak the truth. Not the whole truth, because there is no way to say it all. Saying it all is materially impossible: words fail. Yet it is through this very impossibility that the truth holds onto the real" (Lacan 1990, 3). And this point where "truth holds onto the real" is precisely the point involved in formalization. Formalization is not a truth about the Real, but concerns the point of entanglement of speech (as sustaining the dimension of truth) with the Real.

And here we come to the core of the difference between Lacan and Badiou, as Badiou sees it: what makes Lacan an antiphilosopher (or sophist) is his claim that we cannot speak *about* the Real (and that there is no truth *about* the real),[16] and that the Real does not allow for metalanguage. However, on the basis of what has been said so far, we can already see the crucial difference that separates Lacan from, for example, the Wittgensteinian version of this claim. We cannot speak about the Real because speech is *too close to it*, because it can never fully escape the Real, but holds onto it. This is why, instead of the prohibition of the impossible, which we find in Wittgenstein ("whereof one cannot speak, thereof one must be silent"—the famous lines from his *Tractatus Logico-Philosophicus*), we have in Lacan its double reversal: go on, speak about *anything whatsoever*, and with a little luck and help (from the analyst) you will sooner or later stumble against the Real, and get to formalize (write) it. The Real is not some realm or substance to be talked about, it is the inherent contradiction of speech, twisting its tongue, so to speak. And this is precisely *why there is truth*, and why, at the same time, it is not possible to say it all.

> ... one needs to accept that we speak of truth as a fundamental position, even though we don't know it all, since I define it with the fact that it is only possible to half say it. (Lacan 2011, 173)

This is a quote from 1972, testifying to the fact that truth remains a central category also in "late" Lacan. And, as I have also pointed out, it is through this impossibility of saying it all that the truth holds onto the Real. Paradox is another indicator of this impossibility; it indicates that language cannot be neatly separated from the Real (*about* which it would supposedly speak). And the *place/position* of truth is the point where speech "slips," "lapses" into the Real that it tries to articulate. It is not simply that this Real can be *"felt"* (experienced or "monstrated") only as the limit of the discourse—it is possible to formalize it. This is what Lacanian mathemes are all about. A matheme is not simply a formalization of some reality; rather—and as Lacan himself puts it— it is the *formalization of the impasse of formalization.*

What is thus crucially important to point out is that for Lacan, it is not simply *formalization as such* that is interesting. What is interesting are the impasses (paradoxes) it produces—as points of its own *impossibility* which can themselves be "formalized." And this is precisely why logic (and especially modern mathematical logic) is such an important reference for him: because it makes this double move possible.

> This examination of the logics is not simply interrogation of that which sets its limit to the speech in its apprehension of the Real. In the very structure of this effort to approach the Real, in the very handling of this structure, the latter shows that which of the Real has determined the speech. (Lacan 2011, 20)

It would be difficult to put it more precisely: the structure that attempts to articulate the Real is determined in its foundation by the Real it attempts to formulate. Yet this very determination, far from discrediting in advance all approaches to the Real by way of the structure, is precisely what can make them credible. It is this very determination that can eventually ground (or justify) the psychoanalytic claims to realism.[17] This grounding of realism can take place only from a certain folding of the structure upon itself, and from a singular perspective ("looking awry") on this folding. Psychoanalysis is what introduces this singular perspective.

From its very beginning, logic has advanced by articulating paradoxes. Lacan reminds us of this in "L'étourdit": "I will simply recall that no logical development, this starting before Socrates and from elsewhere than in our tradition, ever proceeded except from a kernel of paradoxes" (Lacan 1973, 49). Yet he does not consider these paradoxes as the limit of rationalist endeavors, as proof of how the Real is inaccessible to discourse, or as proof of the uselessness and arbitrariness of the concept of truth; on the contrary, he takes them as that which can ground rationality, what testifies to the irreducible link between the discursive and the Real, and that which alone opens the space of truth as a fundamental position.

Psychoanalysis does also not simply "side with" the scientific advances made by solving these paradoxes, but accompanies them by producing a singular perspective on them; it formalizes what makes these advances necessary, it formalizes the impasses of formalization. This is why "analytical discourse is not scientific discourse, it is a discourse to which science provides its material, and that is something considerably different" (Lacan 2011, 141).

The specificity of the Lacanian notion of formalization, which is not simply scientific formalization, should also be pointed out in response to a criticism of his method that one sometimes hears: if formalization actually writes something that cannot be said (better) in any other way, are the eventual explanations of these formulas and schemes, then, utterly misguided? If that which is "said" by a formula can be verbalized without loss, unraveled into simple prose, why use formulas at all? If, however, it is not possible to do this, then all "translations" of formulas into prose introduce, conceptually speaking, an irreversible loss.

Just as in the case of the relationship between equivocity and formalization, the answer is that we should not oppose formulas and verbalization. Lacan does not resort to formulas in order to avoid the ambiguities of everyday speech and make sure that there is only one possible meaning to them, but sees the formulas as related to the very logic (and dialectic) of the verbal, insofar as the verbal is inherently inseparable from the negativity that generates it. That is why we can gain as much (or even more) by verbalization of the formal as by a formalization of the impasses of the verbal. There are legendary stories circulating about how Lacan, in his last seminars, almost stopped talking—instead he would make some of his famous knots, and simply throw them to the audience. This indeed conveys the image of a wise man who lost all confidence in words and opted for a "higher" and more reliable mode of communication. Or else, as suggested by Jean-Claude Milner,[18] it conveys the image of a man who relied on topology as a means of destroying language. Yet both these images are somehow at odds with the following explicit statement, also belonging to the repertoire of Lacan's late work (1975): "I do not use knots because they are non-verbal. On the contrary, I try to verbalize them" (Lacan 1976, 35). True, this verbalization could itself be seen as a destruction of language, or as a means of its destruction—or as a pathway to a fundamentally different kind of language. Lacan's late *hommage* to Joyce could be seen as going in this direction. Yet I share the conviction of many of my friends (starting with Badiou) that Beckett is a more compelling, and probably more Lacanian, author than Joyce. We can get a much better idea of what "verbalizing the knots" may amount to by reading Beckett than by reading Joyce. We may also get a better idea of how "boring holes" in language relates to equivocity. Commenting on Beckett's decision to write in French instead of in his mother tongue, Mladen Dolar wrote:

> The first decision that followed from the revelation was to start writing in French and thus to escape the "Anglo-Irish exuberance and automatisms," but this involved a lot more: to escape the tentacles of the mother tongue as the seemingly natural home ground of self-expression, of one's cultural heritage, the territory of the spontaneous and the homely. The mother tongue is not an ally but a foe. But this only leads to this wider claim: language is not an ally but a foe. To write in a language where one is not at home is just a consequence of the fact that one is never at home in a language, so that mother tongue, and ultimately language as such, is but a refuge against what literature ought to do. *To bore holes in language*, as he famously put it in the letter to Axel Kaun.[19]

As we have seen, the Beckettian formulation "to bore holes in language" does indeed resonate strongly with, and in, (the late work of) Lacan. It is also directly related to the issue of equivocity: Dolar also reminds us how, in a wonderful pun, Beckett once said: "En français on est si mal armé": one is so poorly equipped in French as a foreign speaker, but there is Mallarmé lurking behind even the simplest expressions.

This is indeed a perfect example of equivocity that can function as a formula. It could even be considered as the *formula of the very inseparability of equivocity and formalization*. This Beckettian pun is also exactly of the kind used, or practiced, by Lacan. For there are puns and puns, and there are different ways of "using" them. Lacan tends to use them as "formulas," and there is actually a very interesting proximity between his and Beckett's usage of puns.

Earlier on I suggested that psychoanalysis does not resolve the contradiction but, rather, its (symptomatic) solution. It is now time to ask if this is simply a kind of practical bottom line of psychoanalysis? That is: is there a fundamental (structural) impossibility or contradiction which is irreducible, and all we can do is circumscribe or recognize it as such and accept it, in order to prevent it from secretly feeding our pathological fantasies? This is indeed the bottom line in a certain ("liberal") understanding of psychoanalysis. However, I do not think one should endorse this perspective, but rather insist that, no, this is not the bottom line. On the contrary: it is not about accepting the contradiction, but about *taking one's place in it*. This is what the "position of truth" could be understood to amount to. (And let us not forget that in analysis, formalization relates to a shift in our position—otherwise it does not work, and is not "the right formalization," as Lacan also puts it.) Yet this shift of perspective does not occur in the movement that would go from the surface toward the foundation (contradiction as foundation). Rather, the foundation *appears* (takes place) as a splitting of the surface itself. That is to say: the fundamental contradiction appears to be inherent to the terms involved in it. This, for example, is precisely what the Lacanian formulas of sexuation force us to think: not the contradiction between "opposite" sexes, but the contradiction inherent to both, "barring" them both from within.

When I talk about a "fundamental contradiction" I am not referring to some contradiction buried deep down in the foundation of things, and influencing them from there. Contradiction is "fundamental" in the sense that it is persistent, and repeating—yet always in concrete situations, on the surface of things and in the present. It is by engaging with it in these concrete situations that we work with the "fundamental contradiction."

Contradiction is not something that we simply have to accept and "make do with"; it can become, and be "used" as, the source of emancipation from the very logic dictated by this contradiction. This is what analysis ideally leads to: contradiction does not simply disappear, but the way it functions in the discourse structuring our reality changes radically. And this happens as a result of our fully and actively *engaging in the contradiction*, taking our place in it.

CHAPTER 4

OBJECT-DISORIENTED ONTOLOGY

REALISM IN PSYCHOANALYSIS

Many recent philosophical discussions have been marked, in one way or another, by the rather spectacular relaunching of the question of realism, triggered by Quentin Meillassoux's book *Après la finitude* (2006), and followed by a broader, albeit much less homogeneous, movement of "speculative realism." We are witnessing a powerful revival of the issue of realism, with new conceptualizations or definitions of the latter, as well as of its adversary ("correlationism" in place of the traditional nominalism). "Realist ontologies" are emerging faster than one can keep track of them, and we can take this acceleration of realism as an opportunity to raise the question of whether—and how—the conceptual field of Lacanian psychoanalysis is concerned in this debate, considering that the concept of the Real is one of the central concepts of Lacanian theory.

As a quick general mapping of the parameters of this discussion, let me just very briefly recall Meillassoux's basic argument. It consists in showing how post-Cartesian philosophy (starting with Kant) rejected or disqualified the possibility for us to have any access to being outside of its correlation to thinking. Not only are we never dealing with an object in itself, separately from its relationship to the subject, there is also no subject that is not always-already in a relationship with an object. The relation thus precedes any object or subject; the relation is prior to the terms it relates, and becomes itself the principal object of philosophical investigation. All contemporary (post-Cartesian) philosophies are variations on philosophies of correlation. As Meillassoux puts it:

> Generally speaking, the modern philosopher's "two-step" consists in this belief in the primacy of the relation over the related terms; a belief in the constitutive power of reciprocal relation. The "co-" (of co-givenness, of

co-relation, of the co-originary, of co-presence, etc.) is the grammatical particle that dominates modern philosophy, its veritable "chemical formula." Thus, one could say that up until Kant, one of the principal problems of philosophy was to think substance, while ever since Kant, it has consisted in trying to think the correlation. Prior to the advent of transcendentalism, one of the questions that divided rival philosophers most decisively was "Who grasps the true nature of substance? He who thinks the Idea, the individual, the atom, the God? Which God?" But ever since Kant, to discover what divides rival philosophers is no longer to ask who has grasped the true nature of substantiality, but rather to ask who has grasped the true nature of correlation: is it the thinker of the subject–object correlation, the noetico–noematic correlation, or the language–referent correlation? (Meillassoux 2008, 5–6)

The inadequacy of this position is revealed, according to Meillassoux, when it is confronted with "ancestral statements" or "arche-fossils": statements produced today by experimental science concerning events that occurred prior to the emergence of life and of consciousness (for example: "The earth was formed 4.56 billion years ago"). They raise a simple and still, according to Meillassoux, insoluble problem for a correlationist: How are we to grasp the meaning of scientific statements bearing explicitly upon a manifestation of the world that is posited as anterior to the emergence of thought, and even of life—posited, that is, as anterior to every form of human *relation* to that world? From the correlationist point of view these statements are, strictly speaking, meaningless.

One of the great merits of Meillassoux's book is that it has (re)opened not so much the question of the relationship between philosophy and science as the question of *whether they are speaking about the same world*. Alain Badiou has recently raised—or, rather, answered—a similar question in the context of politics: "There is only one world." Yet this question is also pertinent to the issue of epistemology's, or science's, relation to ontology. It may seem in fact as if science and philosophy have been developing for some time now in parallel worlds: in one it is possible to speak of the Real in itself, independently of its relation to the subject, whereas in the other this kind of discourse is meaningless. So, what do we get if we apply the axiom "There is only one world" to this situation? Instead of taking the—on the side of philosophy—more common path, criticizing science for its lack of reflection upon its own discourse, Meillassoux takes another path: the fact that certain scientific statements escape its "horizon of sense" indicates that there is something wrong with philosophy. It indicates that, in order to ensure its own survival as a discursive practice (one could also say: in order to ensure the continuation of metaphysics by other means), it has sacrificed far too much, namely, the Real in its absolute sense.

One should perhaps stress, nevertheless, that this less common path is becoming a kind of trend in contemporary philosophy, and Meillassoux shares it with several authors, authors who are very different in terms of theory. Let us take as an example Catherine Malabou and her philosophical materialism, which—at the time she wrote her book *Les nouveaux blessés*—aimed to develop a new theory of subjectivity based on cognitive sciences. In her polemics with Freudian and Lacanian psychoanalysis she opposes to the "libidinal unconscious," as always-already discursively mediated, the "cerebral unconscious" (autoaffection of the brain) as the true, materialist unconscious (Malabou 2007). Yet if Malabou's materialism moves in the direction of a "naturalization of the discursive," or, more precisely, if it represents an attempt to reduce the gap between the organic and the subject via finding the organic causes of the subject,[1] Meillassoux takes the same path (of reducing this gap) in the opposite direction, via the discursiveness of nature, although he does not go all the way. His realist ontology, differentiating between primary and secondary qualities of being, does not claim that being is inherently mathematical; it claims that it is absolute, that it is independent of any relation to the subject, although only in the segment which can be mathematically formulated. Meillassoux thus preserves a certain gap or leap (between being and its mathematization), without addressing it. The susceptibility of certain qualities to being mathematically formulated is the guarantee of their absolute character (of their being real in the strong sense of the term). Meillassoux's realism is thus not the realism of the universals, but—and paradoxically—the realism of the *correlate* of the universals, which he also calls the referent:

> Generally speaking, statements are ideal insofar as their reality is one with signification. But their referents, for their part, are not necessarily ideal (the cat on the mat is real, although the statement "the cat is on the mat" is ideal). In this particular instance, it would be necessary to specify: the *referents* of the statements about dates, volumes etc., existed 4.56 billion years ago, as described by these statements—but not these statements themselves, which are contemporaneous with us. (Meillassoux 2008, 12)

There seems to be no way around the fact that the criterion of the absolute is nothing but its correlation with mathematics. Not that this implies something necessarily subjective or subjectively mediated, but it surely implies something discursive. And here we come to the core problem of Meillassoux's conceptualizations, which is at the same time what is most interesting about them. I emphasize this as opposed to another dimension of his approach, a dimension enthusiastically embraced by our *Zeitgeist*, even though it has little philosophical (or scientific) value and is, rather, based on free associations related to some more or less obscure feelings of the present "discontent in civilization," to use the Freudian term. Let us call it the psychological dimension, summed up by the following narrative: Since Descartes we have lost the *great Outside*, the absolute outside, the Real, and have become prisoners of our own subjective or *discursive cage*. The only outside we are dealing with is the outside posited or constituted by ourselves or different discursive practices. And there is a growing discomfort, claustrophobia, in this imprisonment, this constant obsession with ourselves, this inability to ever get out of the external inside that we have thus constructed. There is also a political discontent that is put into play here: that feeling of frustrating impotence, the impossibility of really changing anything, of absorbing the small and big disappointments of recent and not-so-recent history. Hence the certain additional redemptive charm of a project that promises again to break out into the great Outside, to reinstate the Real in its absolute dimension, and to ontologically ground the possibility of radical change.

One should insist, however, that the crucial aspect of Meillassoux lies entirely elsewhere than in this narrative, which has detected in him (perhaps not completely without his complicity) the support of a certain fantasy, namely and precisely the fantasy of the "great Outside" which will save us—from what, finally? From that little yet annoying bit of the outside which is at work here and now, persistently nagging, preventing any kind of "discursive cage" from safely closing upon itself. In other words, to say that the great Outside is a fantasy does not imply that it is a fantasy of a Real that does not really exist; rather, it implies that it is a fantasy in the strict psychoanalytic sense: a screen that conceals the fact that the discursive reality is itself leaking, contradictory, and entangled with the Real as its irreducible other side. That is to say: the great Outside is the fantasy that conceals the Real that is already *right here*.

The philosophical core of Meillassoux's project, however, does not consist in opposing the real to the discursive, and dreaming of the breakthrough beyond the discursive; on the contrary, the core of his project is their joint articulation, which would escape the logic of transcendental constitution, and hence of their co-dependence. This joint articulation relies on two fundamental claims: the thesis (mentioned above) about the possible mathematization of primary qualities, and the thesis about the absolute necessity of the contingent. Needless to say, both of these theses are *philosophical*, and aim at laying the foundations for what modern science seems to simply presuppose: namely, and precisely, a shared articulation of the discursive and the real. It would thus seem that they try to adjust the naïve realism of science, replacing it with a reflective, philosophically grounded "speculative" realism.

Yet the first really interesting question is already apparent here: what in fact is the status of the realism which science's operations presuppose? Is it simply a form of naïve realism, a straightforward belief that the nature which it describes is absolute and exists "out there," independently of us? Meillassoux's inaugural presupposition indeed seems to be that science operates in the right way, yet lacks its own ontological theory that would correspond to its praxis. Considering the framework of his project, it is in fact rather astonishing how little time Meillassoux devotes to the discussion of modern science, its fundamental or inaugural gesture, its presuppositions and consequences—that is to say, to the discussion of what science is actually doing. Contrary to this, we can say that Lacan has an extraordinarily well-elaborated theory of modern science and of its inaugural gesture (to some extent this theory is part of a broader structuralist theory of science), in relation to which he situates his own, psychoanalytic discourse. And this is where one needs to start. The relationship between psychoanalytic discourse and science is a crucial question for Lacan throughout his œuvre, even though it is by no means simple. For on the one hand it presupposes their absolute kinship and co-temporality (marked by countless explicit statements like "the subject of the unconscious is the subject of modern science," "psychoanalysis is possible only after the same break that inaugurates modern science"…). On the other hand, there is also the no less remarkable difference and dissonance between psychoanalysis and science, with the concept of truth as its most salient marker, which involves the difference in their respective "objects." In short: the common ground shared by psychoanalysis and science is nothing other than the Real in its absolute dimension, but they have different ways of pursuing this Real.

What is the Lacanian theory of science? In the context of a similar debate, and drawing on the work of Jean-Claude Milner, this question has been recently reopened, and given its full significance, by Lorenzo Chiesa,[2] to whom I owe this part of the discussion. According to this theory, Galileanism replaced the ancient notion of nature with the modern notion according to which nature is nothing other than the empirical object of science. The formal precondition of this change lies in the complete mathematization of science. In other words, after Galileo, "nature does not have any other sensible substance than that which is necessary to the right functioning of science's mathematical formulas" (Milner 2008, 287–288). To put it even more strongly: the revolution of Galilean science consists in producing its object ("nature") as its own *objective* correlate. In Lacan's work we find a whole series of such very strong statements, for example: "Energy is not a substance…, it's a numerical constant that a physicist has to find in his calculations, so as to be able to work" (Lacan 1990, 18). The fact that science speaks about this or that law of nature, and about the universe, does not mean that it maintains the perspective of the great Outside (as not discursively constituted in any way), rather the opposite. Modern science starts when it produces its object. This is not to be understood in the Kantian sense of the transcendental constitution of phenomena, but in a slightly different, and stronger, sense. Modern science literally creates a new real(ity): it is not that the object of science is "mediated" by its formulas; rather, it is indistinguishable from them, it does not exist outside them, *yet it is real*. It has real consequences or consequences in the Real. More precisely: the new Real that emerges with the Galilean scientific revolution (the complete mathematization of science) is a Real in which—and this is decisive—(the scientific) *discourse has consequences*. Such as, for example, landing on the moon. For the fact that this discourse has consequences in the Real does not hold for nature in the broad sense of the word, it holds only for nature as physics or for physical nature. But of course there is always, says Lacan,

> the realist argument. We cannot resist the idea that nature is always there, whether we are there or not, we and our science, as if science were indeed ours and we weren't determined by it. Of course I won't dispute this. Nature is there. But what distinguishes it from physics is that it is worth saying something about physics, and that discourse has consequences in it, whereas everybody knows that no discourse has any consequences in nature, which is why we tend to love it so much. To be a philosopher of nature has never been considered as a proof of materialism, nor of scientific quality. (Lacan 2006a, 33)

Three things are crucial in this dense and decisive quote. (1) The shift of emphasis from a discursive study of the Real to the *consequences* of discourse in the Real; related to this (2) the definition of the newly emerged reality; and (3) the problem of materialism. Let us first briefly stop at the third point, which we have already touched upon in passing with the question of the "cerebral unconscious." At stake is a key dimension of a possible definition of materialism, which one could formulate as follows: materialism is not guaranteed by any matter. It is not the reference to matter as the ultimate substance from which all emerges (and which, in this conceptual perspective, is often highly spiritualized) that leads to true materialism. The true materialism, which—as Lacan puts it with trenchant directness in another significant passage—can only be a dialectical materialism,[3] is not grounded in the primacy of matter nor in matter as first principle, but in the notion of conflict or contradiction, of split, and of the "parallax of the Real" produced in it. In other words, the fundamental axiom of materialism is not "matter is all" or "matter is primary," but relates rather to the primacy of a cut. And, of course, this is not without consequences for the kind of realism that pertains to this materialism.

This brings us to points (1) and (2) of the quote above, which we can take together since they refer to two aspects of this new, "dialectically materialist," realism. The distinction between nature and physics established by Lacan does not follow the logic of distinguishing between nature as an inaccessible thing in itself and physics as transcendentally structured nature, accessible to our knowledge. The thesis is different, and somehow more radical. Modern science—which is, after all, a historically assignable event—creates a new space of the Real or the Real as a new dimension of ("natural") space. Physics does not "cover" nature (or reduplicate it symbolically), but is added to it, with nature continuing to stay where it has always been. "Physics is not something extending, like God's goodness, across all nature" (Lacan 2006a, 34). Nature keeps standing there not as an impenetrable Real in itself, but as the Imaginary, which we can see, like, and love, but which is, at the same time, somewhat irrelevant. There is an amusing story about how some of his friends dragged Hegel to the Alps, in order for him to become aware of, and to admire, the stunning beauty of the scenery there. All Hegel said about the sublime spectacle that was revealed to him is reported to have been: Es ist so (It is so; it is what it is). Lacan would have appreciated this very much. Es ist so; there is nothing more to say about these beautiful mountains. This is not because we cannot really know them, but because there is nothing to know. (If we say that a stone we see is of this or that age, we are talking about another reality—one in which consequences of discourse exist.)

Lacan's definition of this difference is indeed extremely concise and precise. What is at stake is not that nature as scientific object (that is, as physics) is only an effect of discourse, its consequence—and that in this sense physics does not actually deal with the Real, but only with its own constructions. What is at stake is, rather, that the discourse of science creates, opens up, a space in which this discourse has (real) consequences. And this is far from being the same thing. We are dealing with something that most literally, and from the inside, splits the world in two.

The fact that the discourse of science creates, opens up, a space in which this discourse has (real) consequences also means that it can produce something that not only becomes a part of reality, but can also change it. "Scientific discourse was able to bring about the moon landing, where thought becomes witness to an eruption of a real, and with mathematics using no apparatus other than a form of language" (Lacan 1990, 36). To this Lacan adds that the aforementioned eruption of a real took place "without the philosopher caring about it." Perhaps we can see in this remark a problematization of a certain aspect of modern (continental) philosophy, which tends to miss a crucial dimension of science at precisely this point of the Real, and keeps reducing it to the logic of "instrumental reason," "technicism," and so on. We could also see in it a hint at the contemporary coupling of philosophy and "university discourse," the minimal definition of which would be precisely: the social link in which discourse has no consequences.

To return to the starting point of this digression: with regard to the question of realism in science, Lacan's diagnosis could be summed up as follows:

although it may be true that naïve realism constitutes the spontaneous ideology of many scientists, it is utterly irrelevant for the constitution of scientific discourse, its efficiency and its mode of operation. As we have already seen, this means: modern science did not arrive at the absolute character of its referent by relying on the presuppositions of naïve realism, that is, by naïvely assuming the existence of its referent "in nature," but by reducing it to a letter, which alone opens up the space of the real consequences of (scientific) discourse. And the word "reducing" is not to be taken in the sense of reducing the richness of sensible qualities to an absolute minimum, yet a minimum in which we would be dealing with the continuation of the same substance; it should be taken in the sense of a cut, and of substitution. What is at stake also is not the classical logic of representation: the letter does not represent some aspect of sensible nature, but literally replaces it. It replaces it with something that belongs to discourse (to the semblance), yet something that can be—precisely because it belongs to discourse—formulated in the direction of the Real. This brings us back to the point formulated earlier: "It is not worth talking about anything except the real in which discourse itself has consequences" (Lacan 2006a, 31). This is not an argument about the Real being merely the effect of discourse. The link between discursivity and the Real (which is, after all, also what Meillassoux tackles in his polemics with contemporary obscurantism)[4] finds here a much firmer foundation than in the case of simply stating that the referent (a "natural object") is absolute in, and only in, its mathematizable aspect. Meillassoux (and this is a weak point of his argument) does not see the mathematization of science as a cut in reality that (only) produces the dimension of the Real, but as the furthest point of a continuum, of a continuous sharpening of the ways in which scientists speak about reality; and the Real refers to the purely formal/formalizable segment of a thing remaining, in the end, in the net of this sharpened form of scientific speech. Let us recall: "the referents of the statements about dates, volumes etc., existed 4.56 billion years ago, as described by these statements—but not these statements themselves, which are contemporaneous with us." The ideal character of a scientific formula catches in its net, here and now, a fragment of the thing that is in itself absolute (that is to say, which existed as such, and independently of this net, 4.5 billion years ago). Or, to put it another way: the Real is that portion of a substance that does not slip through the net of mathematizable science, but remains caught in it. Lacan's metaphor, and with it his entire perspective, is quite different in this respect: the Real is guaranteed not by the consistency of numbers (or letters), but by the "impossible," that is, by the limit of their consistency. If it is not worth talking about the Real (or Nature) *outside* of discourse, the reason is that we necessarily stay on the level of semblance, which means that we can say whatever we like. The Real, on the other hand, is indicated by the fact that not all is possible. Here we come to the other crucial component of the Lacanian Real, binding the realism of consequences to the modality of the impossible. Together they could be articulated as follows: something has consequences if it cannot be anything (that is, if it is impossible in one of its own segments).

> The articulation, and I mean algebraic articulation, of the semblance—which, as such, only involves letters—and its effects, this is the only apparatus by means of which we designate what is real. What is real is what makes/constitutes a hole [*fait trou*] in this semblance, in this articulated semblance that is scientific discourse. Scientific discourse advances without even worrying whether it is a semblance or not. What is at stake is simply that its network, its net, its *lattice*, as we call it, makes the right holes appear in the right places. It has no other reference but the impossible at which its deductions arrive. This impossible is the real. In physics we only aim at something which is the real by means of a discursive apparatus, insofar as the latter, in its very rigor, encounters the limits of its consistency.
> But what interests *us*, is the field of truth. (Lacan 2006b, 28)

Before addressing this last question of truth, and of what it implies for the relationship between psychoanalysis and science, let us return to the beginning of our considerations. It would not be appropriate to conclude without accepting the challenge of Meillassoux's initial question, in all its estimable directness and simplicity. That is: what does the Lacanian realism of consequences, combined with the impossible, imply for the status of so-called ancestral statements? Does the statement "the earth was formed 4.5 billion years ago" make any sense independently of us; that is: does it refer to a specific *object* which did in fact (albeit according to our way of counting, and based on radiometric dating) exist 4.5 billion years ago?

Why not venture an answer? In order to formulate it I will draw on a very fascinating story, which revolves precisely around fossils and which—if taken in *its* speculative dimension—can give to the notion of arche-fossil a very intriguing Lacanian twist. In his book Meillassoux does in fact at some point hint at this story—but it remains a completely cursory hint, serving only as a rhetorical argument for mocking the absurdities with which correlationism would seem to be compatible, and it misses precisely the speculative potential of the story in question.

In one of his superb essays, entitled "Adam's Navel," Stephen Jay Gould draws our attention to a most astonishing, "ridiculous," yet extremely elegant theory suggested by the renowned British naturalist Philip Henry Gosse (Gould 1985). Gosse was Darwin's contemporary, and he published the work that interests us (*Omphalos*) in 1857, that is, only two years before the publication of Darwin's *On the Origin of Species*. He was a most passionate naturalist, and one of his greatest passions was fossils, which he studied and described with particular devotion. At that time the nascent science of geology had already gathered evidence for the earth's enormous antiquity, which bluntly contradicted its age according to Genesis (6,000 years). And this was Gosse's principal dilemma—for he was not only a dedicated naturalist, but also a deeply religious man. The core of his theory thus consisted of an attempt to resolve the contradiction between the (relatively recent, according to the Bible) creation *ab nihilo*, and the real existence of fossils of a much more venerable age. He came up with a rather ingenious theory according to which God did indeed create the earth about 6,000 years ago, but he did not create it only for the time to come, for the future, but also retroactively, "for the past"—at the moment of creating the earth, he also put the fossils in it. We should not miss the beauty of this self-effacing gesture: God creates the world by effacing the traces of his own creation, and hence of his own existence, to the benefit of scientific exploration. And it is probably no coincidence that the theological world rejected this theory even more passionately than the scientific world did. The Reverend Charles Kingsley, author of *The Water-Babies* and a friend of Gosse, was asked to review Gosse's book. Refusing, he wrote to Gosse:

> Shall I tell you the truth? It is best. Your book is the first that ever made me doubt, and I fear it will make hundreds do so. Your book tends to prove this—that if we accept the fact of absolute creation, God becomes *Deus quidam deceptor* ["God who is sometimes a deceiver"]. I do not mean merely in the case of fossils which *pretend* to be the bones of dead animals; but in the one single case of your newly created scars on the pandanus trunk, your newly created Adam's navel, you make God tell a lie. It is not my reason, but my *conscience* which revolts here....I cannot...believe that God has written on the rocks one enormous and superfluous lie for all mankind. (Quoted from Hardin 1982)

Indeed, the consensus opined that God could not have "written on the rocks one enormous and superfluous lie." According to Gould, modern American creationists also mostly, and vehemently, reject this theory for "imputing a dubious moral character to God."

The interest of Gosse's theory for our discussion consists above all in pointing out the insufficiency of a simply linear theory of time with respect to the question of the Real. Also, the patina of bizarreness that surrounds Gosse's story should not blind us to the fact that, structurally speaking, his dilemma is exactly Meillassoux's. We have only to replace God's creation with human creation (nature as subjectively/discursively constituted), and we get a strangely similar question: does science study only something which we have ourselves constituted as such, posited (as external), or is this exteriority independent of us, and has it existed exactly as it is since long before us? The Lacanian answer would be: it is independent, yet it *becomes* such only at the very moment of its discursive "creation." That is to say: with the emergence—*ex nihilo*, why not?— of the pure signifier, and with it of the reality in which discourse has consequences, we get a physical reality independent of ourselves. (Which, to be sure, is not to say that we do not have any influence on it.) And of course, this independence is also gained for the time "before us." The reality of arche-fossils or objects of ancestral statements is no different from the reality of objects contemporary with us—and this is because neither the former nor the latter are correlates of our thinking, but are instead *objective correlates of the emergence of a break in reality as a homogeneous continuum* (which is precisely the break of modern science, as well as the break of the emergence of the signifier as such). This is the very reason why Lacan's theory is indeed "dialectically materialist": the break implies nothing other than a speculative identity of the absolute and of becoming. They are not opposed, but need to be thought together. Something can (in time) *become absolute* (that is, timeless). The absolute is *at the same time* both necessary and contingent: there is no absolute without a break/cut in which it is constituted as absolute (that is to say, as "necessarily necessary"— whereby this redoubling is precisely the space in which discourse has consequences), yet this break itself is contingent.

Meillassoux's gesture, on the other hand, consists in absolutizing contingency as the only necessity. In this way he ultimately subscribes to the logic of constitutive exception which totalizes some "all": all is contingent, all but the necessity of this contingency. Unlike this logic of constitutive exception, Lacan's axiom could be written as "the necessary is not-all." It does not absolutize contingency, but suggests that contradiction is the point of truth of the absolute necessity: the absolute is at the same time both necessary and contingent.

And this finally brings us to the crucial difference that nonetheless exists between psychoanalysis and science, and which Lacan keeps relating to the question of truth, staring from his famous 1965 essay "Science and Truth," where we read:

> The fact is that science, if one looks at it closely, has no memory. Once constituted, it forgets the circuitous path by which it came into being; otherwise stated, it forgets a dimension of truth that psychoanalysis seriously puts to work. (Lacan 2006c, 738)

As he further specifies, this is not simply about past structures, accidents, or even mistakes that often pave the way for huge scientific breakthroughs (resolving a "crisis"), it is about the subjective toll (*le drame subjectif*) that each of these crises takes (Lacan mentions J. R. Mayer and Cantor). However, the subject here is not simply the one who comes up with this or that new idea, it is what emerges in the *discontinuity* that defines scientific advances. If science has no memory, it has no memory of that out of which emerges the objective status of its enunciations. Once again, this is not about scientific truths being necessarily subjective (or about going against the claim that scientific statements hold regardless of who by, why, or how they are enunciated): this "subjective toll" is not something that—had it not been forgotten—would have in any way changed or influenced the *objective* status of the claims. What falls out (of memory) is simply this: at the core of every significant scientific breakthrough there is a radical *discontinuity* which establishes the absolute ("eternal" or timeless) status of its objects; and subject is the name of this discontinuity. As Lacan put it in the same essay, "the subject is, as it were, internally excluded from its object" (Lacan 2006c, 731). This is precisely the subject that carries the dimension of truth which psychoanalysis "puts to work."

And this is what is nicely captured in Gosse's story if we shift the picture just a little bit: science is the God who, in creating reality, cannot but efface the traces of his own creation, the God who "has no memory." This is what "the subject of the unconscious is the subject of modern science" means. Written on the rocks is not one enormous lie; that science creates its object does not mean that this object did not exist before this creation, and that hence the "ancestral statements" or "arche-fossils" are simply meaningless; it means that the absolute character of the existence of "arche-fossils" is the *very form* of absolute contingency. Psychoanalysis claims that the reality of (signifying) creation comes with an unexpected addition: the unconscious. The unconscious is proof of the existence of the contingent; it is where something of which we have no memory continues to work as truth. What this truth testifies to first and foremost is the *cut* through which all that is "meaningful," or that is said to be "true" or "false," is created. For example—and if we jump back to science—this also implies that no amount of "plasticity of the brain" can smooth out, or avoid the cut involved in, the signifiers capable of producing a plausible scientific theory of this same "plasticity." It cannot do away with this cut without losing its own *real* and falling instead straight into yet another *Weltanschauung* or "world-view." For the brain, as a meaningful referent of science, is not the piece of meat in our heads, but an object such that scientific apparatus has consequences for it (and in it). This is what "brain sciences" often tend to forget, and what the subjects of the unconscious remind us of.

HUMAN, ANIMAL

Let us now continue our investigation by turning our attention to the philosophical category of the "human animal," and interrogating the kind of differentiating mapping it implies. Philosophically speaking, the question of the human animal has always been based on double difference. There is, first, the difference that is supposed to distinguish us as humans (be it reason, language, using tools...). On a first level, this difference can be taken just as any other difference that differentiates one animal species from others. From this perspective, humans have a (properly differentiated) place within the animal kingdom; we can put them there, on the evolutionary tree, together with other animals, in all their specificity (and in spite of it). This is a first-level difference, which one could call inclusive, in the sense that it *allocates* us our own proper place within a differential (animal) structure. We are a specific kind of animal called "humans" (or human animals).

The tricky (and controversial) question only begins here, and could be formulated as follows: Is human difference a different kind of difference? This is the question of the "human exception," which is usually posited in self-referential (self-differential), and not simply differential terms. The question of whether we are also something other than just another kind of animal always seems to mobilize the divide, not simply between ourselves and animals, but also between ourselves as animals, and ourselves as something else: between ourselves as "human animals" (say, as functioning on the level of basic "animal" needs) and ourselves as something more, or other. That is to say: as human beings, we are not different from animals as "whole beings"; we are partly animals, and partly something very different, even entirely different. The body/spirit difference is the prototype of this configuration, also in its laicized version. In this configuration, the distinction and superiority of the second term is usually testified to by its ability to ignore, or even to turn actively against, the first term, which binds us to animality.

Within this general framework there seem to be two dominant ways of conceiving what human "animality" refers to. In the first, the animal (as in "human animal") is cast as the figure of an *untamed excess*. This idea is rooted above all in a specific aspect of the Christian imaginary which, at the same time, invented autonomy of the excess and cast it as sin, "outsourcing" it, so to speak, to the other in us (the animal). Not that it has much to do with how animals behave; to "behave like an animal" can refer here to any kind of human "weakness" understood as an incapacity to control, tame, or suppress that excess. This is the image of an unrestrained, excessive enjoyment.

Somewhat directly opposed to the figure of an untamed excess is the figure of animality as *lacking any (real) excess*. I would say that this is a predominantly modern figure of the human animal: an organic (and/or symbolic) system closed upon itself, entirely "lawful," unable to do something *more* than be an extension of "natural causality," not being ridden with some kind of excessive restlessness, being-toward-death (Heidegger), *jouissance* (Lacan), capacity of truth based on *excès errant* (Badiou)....

The first example of this modern figure that comes to mind is, of course, Kant. What he calls in his practical philosophy "pathological," nonethical actions are simply actions of the "human animal." They do not imply any kind of spectacular, excessive, or "bestial" crimes; their basic "crime" is that they do nothing but conform to the law (of natural causality, that is, of the "human animal"). For example—and this is well known: if we do something right, but do it out of fear, including fear of God, we act as human animals, not as ethical subjects. To qualify as ethical subjects, it is not enough that we conform to the moral law—what is needed is that additional, excessive "only because of the law," which alone indicates for Kant that something other than natural causality could indeed be at work. In other words, the properly human, the "human human," is on the side of the excess, including the excessiveness of the moral law itself, interrupting natural causality.

It is probably not surprising that Nietzsche suggests yet another perspective which, to some extent at least, comes close to what Freud and Lacan seem to propose: namely, that the problem with the "human animal" is that it is not "fully" what it is supposed to be. In other words, the problem with humans is not that they are half animals and half something else, but that they are half animals, full stop. Not only is there nothing but the animal part, even this part is not "whole," but lacks something. And the difference (all the "superstructure" of humanity) is generated at the point of this lack. It is generated as a disguise, as clothing for this lack, for this failure to be fully animal.

Let us look at a few passages from the paragraph entitled "How morality is scarcely dispensable" from *The Gay Science*:

> A naked human being is generally a shameful sight....Suppose that, owing to some magician's malice, the most cheerful company at table suddenly saw itself disrobed and undressed; I believe that...their cheerfulness would vanish and that the strongest appetite would be discouraged—it seems that we Europeans simply cannot dispense with that masquerade which one calls clothes.
>
> Now consider the way "moral man" is dressed up, how he is veiled behind moral formulas and concepts of decency—the way our actions are benevolently concealed by the concepts of duty, virtue, sense of community, honorableness, self-denial—should the reason for all this not be equally good? I am not suggesting that all this is meant to mask human malice and villainy—the wild animal in us; my idea is, on the contrary, that it is precisely as *tame animals* that we are a shameful sight and in need of moral disguise....The European disguises himself *with morality* because he has become a sick, sickly, crippled animal...; for he is almost an abortion, scarce half made up [*etwas Halbes*], weak, awkward. (Nietzsche 1974, 259)

Nietzsche speaks of man *becoming* such, and of becoming such in a certain geographical location (Europe), which seems to suggest that—somewhere, not here, sometime, not now—there existed a real, "whole" (human)

Animal.... Without endorsing this perspective, I would simply like to retain the powerful image of "man" as *etwas Halbes*, as an animal aborted before it was "finished." And of culture and morality as taking place at, or as anchored precisely in, this point of ontological incompleteness of being-animal, rather than something that exists for the purposes of "taming" or hiding the wild animal in us. This is not the image of man as half animal and half something else, but of man as a being the animal part of which is lacking something, and of "humanity" appearing as the dress (disguise) to cover up this lack, this missing part. The image is interesting because it does not suggest simply a kind of (vulgar) evolutionist notion of that what is properly human as prosthesis, complementing a deficiency/weakness, making up for it, like an artificial leg replacing a missing organic leg, for instance. The image suggests something different: veiling, dressing up the missing part, which is to say: inventing/producing "humanity" *on* and *around* this void (around the nonexistence of the Animal), without eliminating it or filling it out (as an artificial limb or organ would). A half-animal is dressed up (there is no direct continuity between it and the dress, but an irreducible gap), and now this dress itself becomes the *site* of (further) development, the invention of humanity and of the eventual excess.

What (Lacanian) psychoanalysis brings to this debate about the human animal shares something with the Nietzschean suggestion: there is no "human animal" understood as a fully operative and self-sustaining animal entity in men. *There is no* animal, zero level of humanity ("human animal") which, left to itself, would function on a kind of autopilot of survival or self-preservation. There is no zero level of the human (animal), as a quasi-neutral basis, from which a human being would then eventually diverge and rise toward higher and properly human aspirations and accomplishments. The human animal is a half-finished animal, that is to say, an animal that does not work/function as it is supposed to. The plus (what in human is more than animal) takes the place of the less (what in human is less than animal).

At its most general level, the psychoanalytic theory of the drives (as different from instincts) is precisely a conceptualization of deviations at work already at this supposed zero level of organic functions, needs, and their satisfaction. As I emphasized in earlier chapters (and have elaborated in more detail elsewhere),[5] the concept of the drive (and of its object) is not simply a concept of the deviation from a natural need, but something that casts a new and surprising light on the nature of human need as such: in human beings, any satisfaction of a need allows, in principle, for another satisfaction to occur, which tends to become independent and self-perpetuating in pursuing and reproducing itself. There is no natural need that is absolutely pure, that is to say, devoid of this surplus element which splits it from within. Drive can neither be completely separated from biological, organic needs and functions (since it originates within their realm, it starts off by inhabiting them), nor simply reduced to them.

This independent life of the drives and their own autonomous logic, which further combines with different things, ideas, and objects, this satisfaction beyond need, or pleasure beyond pleasure, is what Lacan refers to as enjoyment (*jouissance*). And it is here that he situates the difference between "animal" and "human." He says, for example: "If an animal eats regularly, it is clearly because it doesn't know the enjoyment of hunger" (Lacan 2011, 54).

This is also the point that Lacan makes in relationship to Heidegger and his *Sein-zum-Tode*, being-toward-death, which defines the human difference for him. It could be considered a properly Lacanian intervention into a significant contemporary philosophical debate. What is the status of death in Heidegger's being-toward-death? If death is not basically trivial, this is for the simple reason that our awareness and relationship/attitude to it make all the difference, and open up the metaphysical dimension proper. To put it very simply: because of death, it matters how we are and live, what we do. Žižek was right to point out, in this context, how it would be wrong to read the "being-toward-death" and, more generally, the theme of human finitude in contemporary philosophy simply as a morbid obsession with what makes man equal to and thus reduced to a mere animal; to read it as blindness to that properly metaphysical dimension that eventually allows man to gain "immortality" in a specifically human way. This kind of reading ignores a crucial point made by Heidegger apropos of Kant's critical break: the very space for the specific "immortality" in which human beings can eventually participate is opened up by man's unique relationship to his finitude and the possibility of death. What is thus at stake (with this theme of "finitude" and being-toward-death) is not that it denies the specifically human mode of "immortality"; rather, it reminds us that this "immortality" is based precisely on the specific mode of human finitude (Žižek 1999, 163).

Where this question is concerned, there is no doubt that Lacan belongs to the post-Kantian perspective as formulated by Heidegger. The shift (and with it a very important difference with respect to Heidegger) occurs at another point, and the simplest way to formulate it is perhaps the following: the structural place occupied, in Heidegger, by *death* (as the very mode of human finitude that grounds specifically human immortality), becomes with Lacan the real of enjoyment, *jouissance*. Lacan's point here is extremely precise and at the same time far-reaching: it is not simply our attitude toward (the possibility of) death that opens up the space of the specifically human dimension (for example, the possibility of actions which are not reducible to the causality of the positive order of Being, to this or that calculation of pleasures); rather, it is the fact that we are situated within an (unsought) portion of enjoyment that makes different attitudes toward death possible to begin with. Death as such, in itself, does not yet involve the possibility of a "dramatic" relationship to itself; this relationship becomes "dramatic" only when *jouissance* intervenes:

> The dialog of life and death...becomes dramatic only from that moment when enjoyment intervenes in the equilibrium of life and death. The vital point, the point where...a speaking being emerges is this disturbed [*dérangé*] relationship to one's own body which is called *jouissance*. (Lacan 2011, 43)

Lacan's point here could be summed up as follows: the relationship between life and death is indeed trivial, or would indeed be trivial, if it were not always- already interrupted, complicated from within. On a most basic level, *jouissance*, enjoyment as "a disturbed relationship to one's body," refers to the fact that enjoyment, by contaminating, flavoring with enjoyment, the satisfaction of all the body's basic needs, introduces in the (supposed) immediacy of living and of satisfying one's needs a crucial gap, a *décalage*, on account of which things can take a different course than what is supposed to be normal or natural. (Recall: "If an animal eats regularly, it is clearly because it doesn't know the enjoyment of hunger.") *Jouissance* is what breaks up the (supposed) circle of animal life, and wakes us up to metaphysics....

So, the point here is not simply that with human beings enjoyment can be *stronger* than "natural" need and the pursuit of self-preservation; the point is that enjoyment fundamentally modifies the very nature of natural need, splits it from within. We are no longer dealing with the image of some basic (natural) core and a deviation from it—deviations (and their signifying support) are man's *nature*. This is what undermines the classical divide body/spirit— not by simply denying the existence of the spirit, nor by suggesting that it can be deduced from the body (in a linear way), but by suggesting that it can be deduced from something in the body which is not fully there.

In this conception—and differently from Lacan's perspective in his early work—the *jouissance* that "smuggles itself in" in this way is nothing spectacular, it does not refer to any kind of flamboyant transgression. It was in order to emphasize this last point that Lacan coined the notion of surplus-enjoyment (*plus-de-jouir*):

> This is why I'm describing what appears here as "surplus *jouissance*" and not forcing anything or committing any transgression. I beg you to bite your tongue over all this nonsense. What analysis shows, if it shows anything at all...is very precisely the fact that we don't ever transgress. Sneaking around is not transgression. Seeing a door half open is not the same as going through it.... There is no transgression here, but rather an irruption, a falling

into the field, of something not unlike *jouissance*—a surplus. (Lacan 2007, 19–20)

Even in this "modest" version, however, enjoyment is not finitude as closure, irrevocably locking us within the register of "human animal"—here the Lacanian perspective differs, for example, from that of Badiou, who speaks in this respect of "our carnal exposition to enjoyment, suffering and death" (Badiou 2009, 1). Rather—and precisely as something unexpectedly "falling into the field" (of our body)—enjoyment is what disturbs this animal, wakes it up to a different reality, wakes it up to metaphysics (or politics), makes it do all kinds of strange, "human" or inhuman things. Here is another passage from Lacan that states precisely this:

> What, in fact, does it mean to be asleep? It means to suspend what is there in my tetragon, the semblance, the truth, the enjoyment and the surplus-enjoyment. This is what sleep is made for, anyone who has ever seen an animal sleeping can see that—what is at stake is to suspend the ambiguity at work in the relationship of the body to itself, namely the enjoyment (*le jouir*).... When we are asleep, the body wraps itself up, rolls up into a ball. To sleep is not to be disturbed. And enjoyment is disturbing. One is usually disturbed, but when one is asleep, one can hope not to be disturbed. This is why, starting from here, everything else disappears. There is no longer question of the semblance, nor of truth, nor of surplus-enjoyment—since all this is related, it's the same thing. Yet, as Freud tells us, the signifier keeps working during our sleep as well. (Lacan 2011, 217)

And here, with this last remark, we raise of course the properly Freudian question of dreams and of that enjoyment that the working of the signifier smuggles into a dream, which eventually disturbs us—even when we are fast asleep, rolled up into a ball—waking us from within the dream. The edge at play here is the very "rub" upon which Hamlet's famous soliloquy dwells:

> To die, to sleep—
> No more—and by a sleep to say we end
> The heartache, and the thousand natural shocks
> That flesh is heir to. 'Tis a consummation
> Devoutly to be wished. To die, to sleep—
> To sleep—perchance to dream: ay, there's the rub,
> For in that sleep of death what dreams may come
> When we have shuffled off this mortal coil,
> Must give us pause. There's the respect
> That makes calamity of so long life.

What constitutes the problem, makes us twitch and hesitate, is not (the thought of) death, but (the thought of) that which—in the same way as it haunts us in the sleep of life—might haunt us in our sleep of death. What scares us is that even in the sleep of death something might come and disturb us, haunt us, and would not let us (not) be....In precisely this sense, the "death drive" (which, in psychoanalysis, is the conceptual name for this dimension) is not so much something that aims at death as a strange deviation from the supposed homeostasis of death itself. This is what makes the term *undead*, used by Žižek, so appropriate in speaking of the notion of the drive. We could also say that in themselves, life and death are just parts of the same cycle: life as life is not yet a declination from death or the opposite of death; rather, it is its continuation by other means.[6] Or, if life is a declination from death, it is a simple declination; a more consequential declination occurs as declination from declination, which produces a third process: the declination of life from life does not simply produce death, but the "death drive" as something undead that haunts both life and death. Life would indeed be merely a curious extension of death, its own curious detour, if there was not another detour appearing within this detour, another declination that disturbs the sleep of life itself: *jouissance* or the drive.

However, all these important emphases still carry with them a certain problem, or ambiguity. For it seems that with the positing of the drive (and of its constitutive deviation) as that which constitutes the *human exception*, we also lose something essential in the concept of the drive. In order to define this problem better, we can call on the otherwise highly problematic first translations of the Freudian *Trieb*: "instinct" in English, "*instinct*" in French, later substituted by "drive" and "*pulsion*." Their problematic character notwithstanding, these early translations nevertheless indicate a real problem. And, not surprisingly, Lacan was well aware of this.

> Notice the ambiguity that the word "Trieb" has taken on in psychoanalytic stupidity....Its usefulness in analytic discourse would merit our not rushing in and translating it as "instinct." But after all, these slippages do not occur for no reason. And although for a long time I have been emphasizing the aberrant character of this translation, we are nevertheless within our rights to benefit from it. (Lacan 2007, 16)

We could say that these early ("erroneous") translations are not simply or solely the result of a misunderstanding of Freud, but also the result of a real difficulty. It seems indeed that something is irredeemably lost in both translations, "instinct" and "drive." There is no doubt that what Freud discovered and named *Trieb* is not "instinct" in the sense in which we usually speak of "animal instincts"—as a kind of inborn survivalist autopilot aiming at self-preservation.

And it is important to point out this difference. Yet on the other hand, we also risk missing the point if we simply say that drive is something *completely different*, which has nothing whatsoever to do with "nature" or "animal," and if we thus make it the (psychoanalytic) carrier of the "human exception." For this would entail going too far, and jumping over the most difficult and crucial point. What is this point? It is the fact that *Trieb* (or *jouissance*) is precisely neither the one nor the other, neither (the) Animal nor simply (the) Human.

The topology of the drive can in fact be understood in two ways. It could be understood as positing that *with humans* the deviation from organic need (piloting the Animal) is original, and that it is this deviation as original that constitutes the human Difference, Exception. This would be the standard reading. Yet there is also another possible reading, which pushes further and radicalizes this position. This other reading suggests that—as a being of the drive—man is neither part of (organic) nature, nor its exception (nor something in between), but *the point where nature's own inherent impossibility, impasse, gets articulated as such*. In this perspective the difference between human and animal becomes a most peculiar one: "human difference" (or singularity) is what testifies to the fact that its Other (the Animal) does not exist (that it is itself inconsistent, irreducible to a kind of sheer autopilot force of survival). Lorenzo Chiesa[7] has recently brought to our attention a significant shift that occurs between Lacan's early and late work with respect to the question of "animal sexuality." In *Seminar I* Lacan does not hesitate to define it as the efficiently fitting correspondence of a key with a keyhole, hence implying precisely that the Animal exists. On the other hand, *Seminar XIX* warns us that the "supposed animal model" of perfectly bi-univocal reproductive complementarity—"the animal image of copulation [that] seems to us to be a sufficient model of what is at stake in the sexual relationship"—from which we would deviate as a biological exception, is itself nothing but a side effect of the "fantasy of the soul" [*fantasme animique*] through which *we* imaginarily "observe" the animal (Lacan 2011, 96–98).

Yet does this mean that the difference between human and animal (sexuality) simply collapses? Not necessarily. We can still maintain that *jouissance* names something particularly human. Yet this particularly human thing is more like a singularization of a general inconsistency at work in animal life. It is a singleton (in the mathematical sense) of this inconsistency. We could say: whereas animal sexuality is simply inconsistent (and this is what it shares with human sexuality), *jouissance* is something like a set containing this inconsistency as its only element. In other words, what differentiates us from animals is the singling out of the negativity that we may well *have in common*. This is what makes all the difference. And this singling out occurs with the signifier and its logic. In this perspective humans are not exceptions to the animal, nor are they simply animals; rather, they are the question mark to the very notion of the animal as a consistent entity. Humans are, quite literally, the living proof that the Animal doesn't exist.

But one could go even further and radicalize these claims by extending them to "nature" or material reality as such, and suggesting that the deviation from the course of natural laws (or from the norm) is not coextensive with humankind (originating in it), but constitutive for the reality and the norm as such, and synonymous with what Žižek calls the "incomplete ontological constitution of reality." The speaking being is neither part of (organic) nature, nor its exception (nor something in between), but its *Real* (the point of its own impossibility, impasse). The speaking being is the real existence of an ontological impasse. So, what is at stake is not that man is distinguished by the declination from nature and its laws; man is not an exception (constituting the whole of the rest of nature), but the point at which nature *exists* (only) through the inclusion of its own impossibility.

From here it would also follow that the "natural norm" (for example, the unproblematic instinct, homogeneity of the need and its satisfaction, and, even more broadly, biological, chemical, physical laws) is secondary with respect to the "incomplete ontological constitution" of nature. Yet this does not mean that the norm or the laws do not really exist, and that they are simply ways in which man domesticates and thinks what is in itself a chaotic, incomplete nature. The incomplete ontological constitution is not synonymous with chaos. The point I am trying to make would be different: nature in itself is not chaotic, it is "lawful" (in the scientific sense), yet this "lawfulness" is nothing other than the very structuring of its own inner antagonism, contradiction, or "incompleteness." It is its very form. In this sense natural laws exist precisely through the nonexistence of Nature.—And in this perspective it is no coincidence that Galilean physics actually starts with a claim that one could formulate as: "Nature does not exist" (that is: Nature as a meaningful whole does not exist). The lawfulness of Nature (including biological laws) is not the other of nature as inconsistent, but is strictly speaking one with the nonexistence of Nature.

Introducing the notion of the drive has thus led us to some rather daring speculations, and it is certainly no coincidence that the psychoanalytic notion of the drive (and particularly of the "death drive") has arguably the most far-reaching philosophical destiny—not only among Lacanian philosophers, but also, for example, for someone like Deleuze. It is precisely with the notion of the drive that sex reaches deeply into ontological interrogations and works at significantly reshaping them. When Freud first introduced the notion of the death drive, in his essay "Beyond the Pleasure Principle," he was already venturing into what are mostly considered to be wild and highly controversial speculations: speculations which, for that very reason, merit our close attention and consideration.

DEATH DRIVE I: FREUD

Among Lacanian philosophers the notion of the death drive plays a very important and persistent role, usually appearing at crucial points of various conceptual arguments. Despite many clarifications (and examples) of what this notion refers to and names, there is still a lot of confusion surrounding it. It may well be that this confusion mostly comes from the fact that, as far as psychoanalysis is concerned, this notion is and remains something of a construction site. Not that other Freudian notions are simply fully established and fixed, with no possibility of a further conceptual life, but the death drive seems to be particularly lacking some sort of initial or fundamental anchorage. The reason is very simple: what Freud, in "Beyond the Pleasure Principle," first introduces under the term death drive (*Todestrieb*) is not exactly what "we" (I count myself among the Lacanians who frequently work with this notion) mean by it.

By way of example, here first is Freud speculating on the possible origins of what he will call the death drive:

> The attributes of life were at some time evoked in inanimate matter by the action of a force of whose nature we can form no conception.... The tension which then arose in what had hitherto been inanimate substance endeavored to cancel itself out. In this way the first instinct (*Trieb*) came into being: the instinct to return to the inanimate state. (Freud 2001b, 39)

This "instinct," or drive, to regain the supposed original homeostatic, tensionless state, is what he will call the death drive. And here is Žižek on the death drive:

> Death drive means precisely that the most radical tendency of a living organism is to maintain a state of tension, to avoid final "relaxation" in obtaining a state of full homeostasis. "Death drive" as "beyond the pleasure principle" is the very insistence of an organism on endlessly repeating the state of tension. (Žižek 2004, 24)

It is crucial to insist, however, that this is not simply a "misunderstanding" (at best) or a "deliberate fabrication" (at worst), but that there actually exists a psychoanalytic (Freudian) *logic* leading from the first to the second. In this chapter I propose to sketch out this logic, and to do so by a close reading of some parts of "Beyond the Pleasure Principle," which is one of Freud's most intriguing and complex essays (he wrote it in 1920). The essay is in no way "linear," but arguably involves several significant shifts in Freud's position. We will start in the middle, where Freud ventures into some of the most astounding speculative reflections via which he introduces the notion of the death drive. These few pages are worth serious consideration not only because they introduce this notion for the first time, but also because they accomplish an intriguing "deconstruction" of our spontaneous understanding of life (and of vitalism), depriving the notion of life of any kind of ontological consistency or ground. From there I will point out and follow several shifts and contradictions in Freud's essay, in order to propose a construction of a different notion of the death drive, yet one that is implied in the essay at different points, and particularly in the shifts of position and doubts to which he keeps returning. I will argue that the genuine psychoanalytic concept of the death drive is in fact related to phenomena that Freud mostly sees as opposed to his notion of the death drive, namely sexuality ("sexual drives," which he views as "life drives"), and that it is precisely on the ground of sexuality that we find the key to the logic of transition from Freud's original to the Lacanian concept of the death drive.

Let us thus begin in medias res and consider this long and most intriguing passage from "Beyond the Pleasure Principle":

> If we are to take it as a truth that knows no exception that everything living dies for internal reasons—becomes inorganic once again—then we shall be compelled to say that "the aim of all life is death" and, looking backwards, that "inanimate things existed before living ones."
>
> The attributes of life were at some time evoked in inanimate matter by the action of a force of whose nature we can form no conception.... The tension which then arose in what had hitherto been inanimate substance endeavored to cancel itself out. In this way the first instinct came into being: the instinct to return to the inanimate state. It was still an easy matter at that time for a living substance to die; the course of its life was probably only a brief one, whose direction was determined by the chemical structure of the young life. For a long time, perhaps, living substance was thus being constantly created afresh and easily dying, till decisive external influences altered in such a way as to oblige the still surviving substance to diverge ever more widely from its original course of life and to make ever more complicated détours before reaching its aim of death. These circuitous paths to death, faithfully kept to by the conservative instincts, would thus present us today with the picture of the phenomena of life. (Freud 2001b, 39)

What is Freud saying here? Viewed from the perspective of the result (everything living eventually dies, and it dies for internal reasons), death appears to be the most fundamental aim of life. Freud suggests a primary character of the death drive (as the drive inherent to life as such), and defines conservative instincts as forces that fortify the detours from this fundamental drive. "Life instincts" (or instincts of self-preservation) would thus not be a kind of affirmative (and spontaneous) force of life, but secondary formations in respect to life's primary drive, which is the death drive. This is a rather astonishing turning around of what constitutes our spontaneous perception: from this Freudian perspective, there is nothing original or spontaneous in the affirmation and conservation of life. Life instincts are automatic (on autopilot), but they are not ontologically primary (for Freud here, there is actually an ontological primacy of, quite literally, "being-toward-death"). Life instincts are a form of "knowledge" (know-how) necessary for the *preservation of this detour* from the fundamental negativity implied in life, which is called death (drive). The death drive names a kind of fundamental or *ontological fatigue* of life as such. It is the steady undercurrent of life in all its colorful and exuberant forms. It is not the opposite of these forms, but it is present in all of them.

As strange as these speculations sound, they should not be dismissed too quickly. Putting into question an automatic (yet problematic, even fantasmatic) presupposition that there exists some kind of original *force* or "will" of life, Freud is able to prepare the ground for a deeply interesting hypothesis. What he says is basically this: life is accidental, and there is no (mysterious) will anywhere that *wants* to live: what we see as "vital forces" are instincts constituted in the process of reiteration of the accident(s) called life. They "know" how to conserve (preserve) the paths of this reiteration, but they don't *want* anything, or aim at anything.

What Freud is saying here is thus actually quite different from the rhetoric of the combat between life instincts and death instincts (which he also uses at some point). This latter rhetoric suggests that there are two independent forces (the "will to live" and the "will to die"), like two Principles struggling with each other. Yet this *makes no sense* if we look closely at what Freud is saying in the passage above. There is no struggle here: life is a circuitous route to death, and conservative instincts are the pavement of this route, they are one with it, indistinguishable from it. They don't "want" anything, they don't "struggle" with death, they simply do their job of making this particular circuitous path to the inanimate operative. Strictly speaking, they work at *maintaining this path*, and not simply at "maintaining life." Freud is more than explicit on this point:

> Seen in this light, the theoretical importance of the instincts of self-preservation, of self-assertion and of mastery greatly diminishes. *They are component instincts whose function is to assure that the organism shall follow its own path to death*, and to ward off any possible ways of returning to inorganic existence other than those which are immanent in the organism itself. (Freud 2001b, 39)

According to this perspective, instincts of self-preservation do not—even temporarily—*change* life's fundamental goal (death), they simply introduce a *temporality* into it. And the mode of this temporality is essentially *repetition*.

Conservative instincts repeat acquired/established paths of life, unless they are forced (for external reasons) to change them; in which case they then tend to repeat these modified paths, and this is what we wrongly perceive as instincts impelling toward change, development, and the production of new forms (Freud 2001b, 37). Nothing is impelling this kind of change—there is no drive to it.

So what is life, if we accept and follow these Freudian reflections and spell out their implications? Life has no ground or source of its own. It is something that happens to the inanimate, it is an accident occurring in the inanimate (possibly due to its own inherent contradiction or inconsistency). It is not simply its other. It is an interruption, a disturbance of the inanimate, a gap appearing in it; or, in another viable speculative perspective: life gives a singular, separate form to an inherent gap on account of which the inanimate does not simply coincide with itself.

In line with the great materialists, and in order to discredit the anthropo-centric (or "correlationist") view of reality, one likes to say that the inanimate is indifferent to life, that it existed long before life occurred, and will exist long after life becomes extinct. Yet what the above considerations invite us to do is to go even a step further. Instead of saying that the (inanimate) universe doesn't give a damn whether we live or die (and that from the perspective of the universe our existence is utterly insignificant), we are invited to consider a possibility which makes us even less exceptional: that we are mere perversions, strange pleasures, of the inanimate itself. Not in the sense of constituting integral, harmonious parts of the great whole or circle of the universe (giving rise to the "oceanic feeling" also discussed by Freud), but in the sense of con-stituting its tics and grimaces.

Life is but a dream of the inanimate. More precisely, it is a nightmare of the inanimate (its nightmarish disturbance), since the inanimate wants nothing but to be left alone. In this sense we could say that the death drive is not so much a drive as an ontological fatigue as a fundamental affect of life—not that it is necessarily experienced, "felt" as fatigue; it is present as a kind of "objec-tive affect" of life....[8]

Hitherto we have been discussing what Freud writes more or less in the middle of his essay. Let us now move to its beginning, where Freud (re)affirms his conviction concerning the primary character of what he named "the pleasure principle":

> In the theory of psycho-analysis we have no hesitation in assuming
> that the course taken by mental events is automatically regulated by the
> pleasure principle. We believe, that is to say, that the course of those
> events is invariably set in motion by an unpleasurable tension, and that it
> takes a direction such that its final outcome coincides with a lowering of

that tension, that is, with an avoidance of unpleasure or a production of pleasure.... We have decided to relate pleasure and unpleasure to the quantity of excitation that is present in the mind but is not in any way "bound"; and to relate them in such a manner that unpleasure corresponds to an *increase* in the quantity of excitation and pleasure to a *diminution*. (Freud 2001b, 7–8)

It is clear from this passage that "the pleasure principle" for Freud does not refer to any kind of hedonistic searching and striving for pleasure, actively looking for gratification and satisfaction, but basically to seeking relief (from tension and excitation), to the "lowering of tension," in an attempt to reach a homeostatic state. If we now relate these opening sentences of Freud's essay to our earlier discussion, it is clear how the "pleasure principle," with its homeostatic tendency, is actually a *mental equivalent* of what appears later on in Freud's speculations as the fundamental tendency of all life to return to the inanimate, and hence to reduce the tension induced (in inanimate matter) by the emergence of life.[9] In this precise sense, and as paradoxical as it may sound, the death drive as first introduced by Freud is in fact simply another name for the "pleasure principle." And when he goes on to describe how the "reality principle" (related to the preservation of life) forces us to make exceptions from the pleasure principle as fundamental, Freud uses the exactly the same image of a detour that he uses later on in the context of discussing the relationship between life and the death drive:

Under the influence of the ego's instincts of self-preservation, the pleasure principle is replaced by the reality principle. This latter principle does not abandon the intention of ultimately obtaining pleasure, but it nevertheless demands and carries into effect the postponement of satisfaction, the abandonment of a number of possibilities of gaining satisfaction and the temporary toleration of unpleasure as a step on the long indirect road to pleasure. (Freud 2001b, 10)

This is exactly the picture we discussed above: life as a disturbance and temporary postponement of what appears as a kind of metaphysical pleasure (homeostasis) of the inanimate. Life/the reality principle is a postponement of death, and of the pleasure principle implied in it. The pleasure principle is synonymous with the death drive, which remains—in spite of detours and temporary postponements—the fundamental goal/principle of life.... There is a direct, *point-by-point mapping* that could be made between the two, between the pleasure principle and the death drive (tendency to return to the inanimate) as present in all life. And just as instincts of self-preservation are not the opposite of the death drive but only its inherent detours, the reality principle is not opposed to the pleasure principle, but functions as its circuitous prolongation. There is strictly speaking no "*beyond* the pleasure principle" to be discerned here. Contrary to what we are inclined to expect, it is thus not Freud's (original) notion of the death drive that corresponds to what goes on "beyond the pleasure principle," and hence to what led Freud to write this essay in the first place (namely, the phenomenon of people clinging on to, and repeating, some *decidedly unpleasant* experiences).

The real opposition appears only in the next step, when Freud—after working with the hypothesis of the death drive as the only drive—introduces what he calls "the true life instincts," which he identifies as sexual. "Sexual drives" (as different from instincts of self-preservation) are now the only drives that seem to break out of the circle of life and death as dominated by the pleasure principle and its fundamental aim to return to the inanimate. They thrive on (at least some) excitement and tension, and are, biologically speaking, related to the "endless" continuation of life, and maintained by its "tension." They also, whether we speak of reproduction (union of two different cells), of love (in all its various forms), or of all great sublimations (such as art), go out of their way and embrace some *alterity*, difference, the Other (or at least a scent of the other). Pleasure (in the Freudian sense), on the other hand, needs no Other; the Other (as Other) is rather disturbing to it....Sexual drives do not so much go *against* the pleasure principle as they seem to suspend it, *invalidate it as a principle* in the first place. They seem to be anti-fatigue, and to have a driving force and logic of their own. It is very important that we keep in mind that this is not simply a driving force of life, but of something singular taking place *within* life. The simple equation of "sexual drives" and "life drives" is thus misleading, since the former rather refer to something in life more (or less) than (just) life.

This is the part of Freud's text where he sets up (after exploring the hypothesis that life's only drive is a death drive) what he himself calls a *dualistic* view, with a clear opposition between *Lebens- oder Sexualtriebe* and *Todestriebe* (an opposition which can be quickly summed up as the opposition between Eros and Thanatos). *Todestriebe* correspond to what we have been discussing so far (to fatigue as life's fundamental and objective affect), whereas sexual drives *split with* this destination and logic, and work in a different direction; they are not just postponements of death, detours on life's path to death: they are detours that make/introduce an actual difference, produce something "new"; they even establish a "potential immortality" (of the species, at the price of the death of individual organisms).

Yet this dualist view also turns out to be unsustainable, and what undermines or complicates it is, to put it very simply, that sexuality cannot be subsumed under the notion of "life instincts." If sexuality corresponded to a "life instinct" there would be no psychoanalysis, for one of its principal discoveries was precisely that there was no fundamental principle (or Law) orienting human sexuality. Moreover, the idea of something (in us) that *aims at* continuation of life, and something that aims at its returning to the inanimate, is not at all what corresponds to the notion of the drive (*Trieb*) proper, which is a much more interesting and complex notion, involving a split, repetition, surplus satisfaction and constant pressure. In a brief reference to Jung that Freud makes at this point, he seems to be reminded of the following fact: the dualism of the drives ("life drives" and "death drives") is actually the other side of conceiving libido as a "neutral," desexualized substance. Jung, he says, "making a hasty judgment, has used the word libido to mean 'instinctual/drive force' (*Triebkraft*) in general."[10] This is precisely what was at stake in his split with Jung, this desexualization of the libido in terms of a neutral primary substance, subsequently divided between different drives which are all part of this "great whole" called the libido, and basically constituting two (complementary) principles.... Freud's fundamental move, on the other hand, was to desubstantialize sexuality: the sexual is not a principle to be properly described and circumscribed, it is the very impossibility of its own circumscription or delimitation. It can neither be completely separated from biological, organic needs and functions (since it originates within their realm, it starts off by inhabiting them), nor can it be simply reduced to them. The sexual is not a separate principle or domain of human life, and this is why it can inhabit all the domains of human life. Ultimately, it is nothing but the inherent contradiction of "life," which in turn loses its self-evident character.

The reference to Jung at this point in the essay seems to remind Freud of this, and actually blows a new and different wind into the sails of his argument. Now we move in the direction of a hypothesis that there are *only sexual drives* (or that all drives are sexual). Nothing follows from psychoanalytic findings, states Freud, that points to any drives other than the libidinal ones, and the libidinal ones are sexual. Freud now inclines toward "monism," but not of the Jungian kind (which is monism of the substance-libido); he inclines toward what I would call the monism (singularity) of antagonism, contradiction, or split. He recognizes this antagonism and split on the ground of sexual drives themselves, and not of "his" death drive, which, as we have seen, is pretty monolithic. For example, the love-object can itself be divided between love and hate, or, as Lacan poignantly formulated it: "I love you, but, because inexplicably I love in you something more than you—the *objet petit a*—I mutilate you" (Lacan 1987, 263). Freud now restates his conviction that all that science can tell us here would amount to the fact that there are only sexual drives. More exactly, that only sexual drives possibly impel us elsewhere than to a return to an earlier (homeostatic) stage. This can be further focused by saying that only sexual drives "*drive*" us in any meaningful sense of the word (differently from the "magnetism of the inanimate," which seems to be of the modality of the *fatigue*, and not of the drive proper—*Trieb*).

Reaffirming his central thesis about the sexual "nature" of the libido as such, Freud, in the last part of his essay, thus works with the hypothesis that there are only sexual *drives*.—Almost imperceptibly, the perspective has thus (again) shifted dramatically. From the monism of the death drive (*qua* pleasure principle) we move to the dualism of Eros and Thanatos (that is, of sexual drives and death drives), and from there to the monism of sexual drives.

In what sense can we say that this now implies a "monism" not of substance, but of a split or an obstacle that prevents substance from being-one? First of all, sexual drives are no longer simply viewed as life drives, because they repeat or reproduce the very split between life and death; with sexual drives death is *inherent* to life, conditioning its perpetuation (and— in brief— this negativity [this "minus"] inherent to life becomes the very site of *psychic* life—insofar as the latter is coextensive with the unconscious).

The repetition of death within sexuated life is pointed at by Freud both on the cellular level[11] and on the level of the individual involved in sexual reproduction.

Lacan explains this as follows:

> We know that sexual division, in so far as it reigns over most living beings, is that which ensures the survival of a species....Let us say that the species survives in the form of its individuals. Nevertheless, the survival of the horse as a species has a meaning—each horse is transitory and dies. So you see, the link between sex and death, sex and the death of the individual, is fundamental. (Lacan 1987, 150)

Lacan often returns to and reaffirms this implication of death at the very heart of sexuation; sometimes in the very terms of "death," and sometimes in the more formal language of "reduction" or "loss" involved in sexual reproduction (for example, when he refers to the joining of two sets of chromosomes).

With sexual reproduction death becomes inherent to life; it is not simply its end or final goal (as in the "return to the inanimate"), but its inherent negativity and internal presupposition. This is precisely the point where another (Lacanian) notion of the death drive starts taking shape, although— as we will see—this split in itself does not yet amount to the death drive proper.

Crucial in understanding the shift from the Freudian to the Lacanian concept of the death drive is thus the (Freudian) concept of sexuality (and its relation to the unconscious). Between Freud insisting that, all things considered, there are only sexual *drives* (or that drives are sexual by definition), and Lacan saying that "every drive is virtually a death drive" (Lacan 2006c, 719), the "missing link" is simply this: death is what lurks in the very midst of sexual drives. Not as their aim, but as a negative magnitude or a minus implied in them, and repeated by them. Let us now attempt to reconstruct the Lacanian notion of the death drive on the basis of Freud's essay.

We can start out from what Freud conceives as *repetition* at work in conservative instincts (instincts of self-preservation): instincts of self-preservation repeat acquired/established paths of life (established detours on its path to death). Instincts repeat the circuitous paths to death (which constitute the phenomena of life as we know them).[12] Now, instead of conceiving the death drive proper as the fundamental omnipresent tendency to return to the inanimate (a kind of magnetism of the inanimate), we have to conceive it as originating in another (kind) of repetition occurring within this "conservative" repetition; as *repetition within repetition*: namely, repetition of some (partial and, so to speak, extracurricular) satisfaction accidentally produced within this conservative repetition. This is very much in tune with how Freud, in "Three Essays on the Theory of Sexuality," deduces sexuality and sexual drives: as a surplus satisfaction/excitation that occurs in the course of the functioning, and satisfaction, of different organic functions. (Like the famous "pleasure of the mouth" occurring in the course of satisfying the need for food.) This surplus is not an external but an internal cause of tension, and of constant pressure; and, paradoxically, the drive originating in this surplus does not aim at lowering or annihilating that tension/excitation, but on the contrary at repeating it, again and again. Moreover, this accidental "extracurricular" satisfaction does not chime with any kind of appeasement, since it is not a satisfaction of a need, and hence not a "calming" of the tension awoken by this need. The dynamic is very different here, because a satisfaction occurs which is not an answer to a preexisting need. Here, the answer precedes the question. And instead of satisfaction producing an appeasement of a surplus excitation, satisfaction (and its repetitions) actually produces, *generates* further *excitation*. Repetition of this surplus satisfaction does in this sense go against the pleasure principle (as the principle of lowering tension), yet not on account of some obscure will to die, but on account of an additional drive that occurs within life itself as its unexpected offshoot.

However—and this is crucial—we must not take this Freudian account to suggest a kind of linear genesis of the (death) drive, in which the latter would simply occur as a direct by-product of the satisfying of organic needs. *Surplus satisfaction itself does not yet qualify as drive.* It is not inconceivable that animals experience some surplus satisfaction when satisfying their needs, yet for it to function as partial object (or object of the drive) this satisfaction must, at the same time, start to function as objective embodiment (object-representative) of the negativity or gap involved in the signifying edifice of being.

This, after all, is the whole point of the *concept* of the death drive. This is what Lacan means when he says that "every drive is virtually a death drive": the death drive is not one among the (partial) drives, but refers to an active split or declination *within every* drive. The death drive points to the negativity around which different partial drives circulate, and which they—in this sense—have in common. This is the split inherent to the drives as such, which is not simply the same as the split of the drive from organic functions. On the one hand there are drives as involved in all kinds of partial surplus satisfactions, following the well-known list (oral, anal, scopic); but there is also the drive as the purely disruptive pulsating negativity that gives them their singular rhythm and torsion. In *Seminar XI*, for example, Lacan emphasizes the difference between object *a* as marking a negativity (loss or gap) as such, around which the drive circulates, and all forms of objects *a*, which "are merely its representatives, its figures" (Lacan 1987, 198). What the drives aim at repeating is not simply the (surplus) satisfaction, but rather this negativity/interruption which can be repeated only by repeating the surplus satisfaction. This is precisely what distinguishes the drive from the "mere auto-eroticism of the erogenous zone" (Lacan 1987, 179).

In other words, as object of the drive the object *a* is always and necessarily double: it is a surplus satisfaction as *sticking to the void* (to the gap in the order of being); that is to say, it is the void and its "crust"—which is also why partial objects function as "representatives" of this void. And this is what allows us to suggest that the real object of the drive is not simply surplus satisfaction (enjoyment or satisfaction as object), but this negativity that "sticks" to it and is repeated by it.

To formulate it in yet another way: we must keep in mind that with the drive we are actually dealing with two different splits (or "deviations"), not just one. There is first the split involved in the surplus satisfaction produced in the course of satisfying organic needs and functions. The repetition involved in the functioning and satisfying of organic functions produces a surplus, unexpected satisfaction, which then becomes the drive of another repetition, repetition within repetition, repeating this surplus satisfaction. And this drive can become stronger than the organic need, in the sense that it now dominates both. This is what seems to be at stake, for example, in gluttony: the surplus satisfaction—surplus in relation to the organic need—produced in the course of consuming food (the pleasure of the mouth, etc....) not only deregulates the organic function, but reverses the causality of this configuration. If the surplus is first a by-product of satisfying the organic need for food, satisfying the organic need for food now becomes a by-product of repeating the surplus satisfaction. And this now functions to the detriment of life (and against lowering tension): not because it wants to destroy life, but because "it" wants to enjoy. This in fact explains one side of the genesis of the object of the drive: there is the object-food, and then there is the satisfaction as object.

But this is not the whole story, nor the only split. It explains the genesis of surplus satisfaction, but it does not explain *why* this surplus satisfaction can have such a "revolutionary" effect, and can amount to a complete reversal of the order of things (or at least to a relative autonomy of the drive with respect to organic functions). Also, it would be much too simplistic to understand gluttony simply as an insatiable striving for surplus satisfaction, for we must also ask what other (symbolic) demand this striving feeds. So: why can surplus satisfaction have such an effect as to amount to a complete reversal of the order of things? As suggested, the answer is: because the structure of the drive implies something else (and more) than this surplus satisfaction: a negativity around which it circulates and which relates (the structure of) the drive to the primal repression: to an inbuilt negativity—negativity transmitted with the "positive" ontological order of being.

We should thus complement Jacques-Alain Miller's thesis according to which the object of the drive is "satisfaction as object"; complement it by specifying that satisfaction becomes object (starts to function as object of the drive) only because it gives body to this negativity, and not simply as satisfaction for the sake of satisfaction. In other words, if the drive wants (us) to repeat the surplus satisfaction, this is not because all it wants is to enjoy.

The drive does not want (us) to enjoy. The superego wants (us) to enjoy. The superego (and its culture)[13] reduces the drive to the issue of satisfaction (enjoyment), making us hostages to its vicissitudes, and actively blocking access to the negativity that drives it. In other words—and this is crucial— satisfaction (for the sake of satisfaction) is not the goal of the drive, but its means. This is what is profoundly disturbing about the "death drive": not that it wants only to enjoy, even if it kills us, but that it wants only to repeat this negativity, the gap in the order of being, even if this means to enjoy. Enjoyment is the means, whereas the "aim" is the repetition of the lack of being in the very midst of being. . . .

Another important point linked to this concerns the relation between surplus satisfaction (or enjoyment) and sexuality. Sexuation itself (sexual reproduction, and the death/negativity implied in it) does not yet amount to what one could call sexuality proper; sexuality proper involves a further step in which the "minus," the negativity involved in sexuation and sexual reproduction, gets a positive existence in partial objects as involved in the topology of the drive. These partial objects are not just "satisfactions as objects," they function at the same time as figures or representatives of that negativity. It is only with this double movement that we progress from sexuation to sexuality proper (a sexuality of speaking beings).

Another way of putting this would be to say that whereas all drives are sexual, there is no sexual drive (as a whole; sexuality is not a totalizing function, it is not what totalizes the drives). There is no "sexual drive" as a whole, and sexuality is driven forward by associations of "partial drives" which have but one thing in common, namely and precisely this "minus" or void. It is the latter that unites them—"unites" them in the sense that it constitutes the gap around which circulate all partial drives while aiming at their different partial objects; and it is this common gap that justifies the fact that these different and diverse polymorphous partial satisfactions are called *sexual*. The partial drives are not simply a *neutral* fragmented multiplicity (with each drive circulating around its partial object), but are "biased" by the negativity they have in common; this negativity gives them their curve. This negativity is "part" of each drive, and it is the one/same in all the drives. Hence the double loop of the drive. (The following diagram is reproduced from Lacan 1987.)

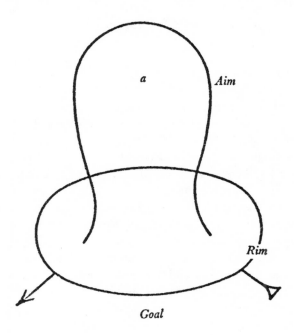

Returning to Freud, and to some of his reflections in "Beyond the Pleasure Principle," we could conclude in the following way. What can eventually shift life's fundamental goal of returning to the inanimate is thus, as paradoxical as this sounds, precisely the death drive. It is the death drive that opens up the space (the scene) of achievements that stretch beyond the ordinary, and beyond business as usual. We have seen how Freud has described instincts of self-preservation as "component instincts whose function is to *assure that the organism shall follow its own path to death*, and to ward off any possible ways of returning to inorganic existence other than those which are immanent in the organism itself." We can now say that the death drive, in our meaning of the term, could be described precisely as establishing (and driving) the ways of returning to inorganic existence *other than those* which are immanent in the organism itself. The organism dies, but it is more than an ideological or religious phrase to say that there are things (creations) that outlive it. And it is precisely at this point that one has to situate the concept of the death drive, and insist on abandoning the idea of the duality of drives: there is only the death drive. Yet it cannot be described in terms of destructive tendencies that want (us) to return to the inanimate, but precisely as constituting *alternative paths to death* (from those immanent in the organism itself). We could say: the death drive is what makes it possible for us to *die differently*. And perhaps in the end this is what matters, and what breaks out from the fatigue of life: not the capacity to live forever, but the capacity to die differently. We could even paraphrase the famous Beckettian line and formulate the motto of the death drive as follows: *Die again, die better!*

TRAUMA OUTSIDE EXPERIENCE

In our discussion of the Freudian death drive so far, we have left out a crucial aspect of "Beyond the Pleasure Principle," the aspect or question that put Freud on the path of writing this essay in the first place: the question of repetition, and particularly of the compulsion to repeat some particularly traumatic incidents. Besides what analysis frequently encounters in the treatment of neurosis, Freud presents a range of different examples of this phenomenon from ordinary life. We come across people, he writes, all of whose human relationships have the same outcome: the benefactor who is abandoned in anger after a time by each of his *protégés*, however much they may otherwise differ from one another; or the man whose friendships all end in betrayal by his friend; or the man who, time after time in the course of his life, raises someone else to a position of great private or public authority and then, after a certain interval, himself overthrows that authority and replaces him with a new one; or the lover each of whose love affairs passes through the same phases and reaches the same outcome. There is also the case that became notorious under the name of *fort–da* (gone–here)—the words used by a small child playing with a wooden reel with a piece of string tied round it, repeatedly casting it away and pulling it back to himself. Even more intriguing are the cases where the subject seems to have a *passive* experience, over which he has no influence, but in which he encounters a repetition of the same fatality. There is the case of the woman who married three successive husbands, each of whom fell ill soon afterward and had to be nursed by her on his deathbed. . . . Even at the level of dreams, which are supposedly fully governed by the pleasure principle and guided by "wish fulfillment," psychoanalysis has discovered a surprising compulsion to repeat some particularly traumatic incidents.

The basic problem presented to psychoanalysis by the compulsion to repeat is therefore as follows: if one starts—as Freud does—from the primary character of the pleasure principle, which aims at the maximization of pleasure (and where pleasure is defined as a "*lowering of tension*") or minimizing of displeasure, then the phenomena of the compulsion to repeat contradict this framework. Why would somebody be compelled to repeat a distinctly unpleasant experience?

This is Freud's explanation: what we find at the origin of repetition is a repression of a traumatic event—repetition appears at the place of remembering; one repeats something one cannot remember. Repetition is thus fundamentally the repetition (in different "disguises") of a concrete, originally traumatic event or experience. Although Freud preserved the basic outline of this explanation, he also saw that it nevertheless leaves several problems and questions unanswered, and he kept returning to these questions. Practically all interesting and productive readings of Freud on this issue emphasize the necessity of another turn which complicates the schema above and puts repetition in a new perspective. Despite some important differences, these readings all agree on one point, which has recently been made again by Ray Brassier in the context of his take on negativity and nihilism: what the compulsion to repeat repeats is not some traumatic and hence repressed experience, but something which *could never register as an experience to begin with*. The trauma which is being repeated is outside the horizon of experience (and is, rather, constitutive of it). This emphasis is absolutely crucial: the trauma is real, but not experienced. And this shifts the debate from the usual framework, which is mostly consumed by the question (or alternative) of the real versus the imagined (fantasized); that is, by the distinction between material reality and psychic reality (fantasy).[14]

Brassier bases his reading on precisely that part of "Beyond the Pleasure Principle" where Freud discusses the death drive in relation to the "return to the inanimate." Since Freud also emphasizes, in a realist manner, that inanimate things existed before living ones, the inorganic, as "initial state" and "aim" of life, cannot simply be understood as a condition internal to the development of life. Just as the reality of the inorganic is not merely a function of the existence of the organic, the reality of the death drive is not merely a function of life's past, or of its future.

> Thus, the repetition which is driven by death does not repeat the latter as though it were an earlier state of affairs experienced by life or consciousness, for the trauma which drives repetition is precisely what cannot be lived or consciously apprehended. Though trauma is real, its reality cannot be calibrated by the life of organism, just as it cannot be commensurate with the resources of consciousness. It can only be registered as a dysfunction of the organism, or as an interruption of consciousness, and it is this dysfunction and this interruption that is repeated. Accordingly, it is because the "originary" traumatic occurrence was only ever registered in the unconscious,

rather than experienced, that there is a compulsion to (re-)experience it. But it can only be re-experienced as something that was neither lived nor experienced, since trauma marks the obliteration of life and experience. Nevertheless, the fact that experience cannot obliterate itself points to the reality of trauma, which cannot simply be constructed as a function of experience. (Brassier 2007, 236)

Fundamentally "traumatic experience" is precisely not an experience, but rather something (a negativity or "scar") that comes, so to speak, as built into the very conditions of our experience, and constitutes the condition of our consequently experiencing something as "traumatic" (in the strong sense of the word).[15] The objectivity of trauma (its independence of our "psychic life") is the very condition of us having a "psychic life" (and experiencing something as "traumatic"). This is an important point in relation to Malabou's criticism of psychoanalysis (Malabou 2007). Malabou's criticism of psychoanalysis is that it cannot conceive of the trauma as real, but only as (necessarily) psychologically mediated. The simplest response to this is that if all trauma is "psychologically mediated," it is precisely because this very *mediation* "comes from the outside," that is, relates to a Real independent of ourselves. Mediation is not a screen separating us from the Real, but is itself partaking in this Real. We could also say: mediation is the trauma (trauma as real). Wounds that are not traumatic in the psychological sense, but simply and directly damage our brain or body, exist of course; yet the question whether a certain wound will also function as "traumatic" (in the psychological sense) depends on another "wound" that is, strictly speaking, outside our experience (starting with our physical experience), because it is one with the constitution of experience.

To return to Brassier—he further substantiates his reading by referring to a passage from Freud's essay in which Freud ventures into intriguing speculations about the genesis of organic individuation, which are also related to our previous discussion of the animate and the inanimate. According to these Freudian speculations, a primitive organic vesicle (that is, a small bladder, cell, bobble, or hollow structure) becomes capable of filtering the continuous and potentially lethal torrent of external stimuli by sacrificing part of itself in order to erect a protective shield against excessive influxes of excitation. In so doing, it effects a definitive separation between organic interiority and inorganic exteriority. The separation between the organic inside and the inorganic outside is thus achieved at the price of the death of part of the primitive organism itself. As Brassier puts it:

> Thus, individuated organic life is won at the cost of this aboriginal death whereby the organism first becomes capable of separating itself from the inorganic outside. This death, which gives birth to organic individuation,

thereby conditions the possibility of organic phylogenesis, as well as of sexual reproduction. Consequently, not only does this death precede the organism, it is the precondition for the organism's ability to reproduce and die. If the death drive *qua* compulsion to repeat is the originary, primordial motive force driving organic life, this is because the motor of repetition— the repeating instance—is this trace of the aboriginal trauma of organic individuation.... The death drive is the trace of this scission: a scission that will never be successfully *bound* (invested) because it remains the *unbindable* excess that makes binding possible. (Brassier 2007, 237–238)

This is a crucial point, and we shall return to it. It isolates a third element in relation to the distinction between life and death (organic and inorganic, animate and inanimate), and "locates" the death drive in this element. There is death which is the opposite of life, but there is also death which preconditions this very opposition, and is presupposed by it. In other words, the death drive is out of joint both in relation to life and in relation to death. It is not an obscure will to return to the inanimate, it is a trace of a trauma that cannot be *experienced* as such, because it is prior to any experience. It is a primordial loss ("minus") which precisely was not capable of being perceived (experienced) as a loss—and in this sense there is nothing "psychological" about this trauma. Let as recall that Freud's original "deduction" of the death drive actually involves a similar configuration: the passage from the inanimate to life involves a loss (of homeostatic state), yet there is nothing (nobody) which could *experience* this loss as a loss: when life comes to life, it is already constituted on the loss of the homeostatic state (of the inanimate), it never lives through this loss. From this perspective, which Freud does not make explicit, there is a loss at the origin of the death drive that could never have been experienced as loss....Only in this perspective can it make any sense to say that "life wants to *return* to the inanimate"; for, strictly speaking, it is only (the interrupted) inanimate that could be said to want to return to the inanimate (as a state it once knew). Life, on the other hand, has nowhere to return to except, precisely, to that which it never had, yet nevertheless lost. That is to say: life has nowhere to return to except that with the lack of which (as built in) it has come to life.

Yet, this important emphasis notwithstanding, Brassier's reading still remains within the classic Freudian schema positing the pleasure principle (*qua* lowering of tension) as the primary principle. In Brassier's genuinely Freudian reading, the compulsion to repeat is in the service of mastering the unbound excess (of excitation) related to the aboriginal trauma, even though the latter could not have been *experienced* as such. The compulsive repetition is thus explained as the mechanism through which "the psyche is striving to muster the anxiety required in order to achieve a successful binding (*Besetzung*) of the excess of excitation released by the traumatic breaching of its defenses. It is this binding that lies 'beyond the pleasure principle'" (Brassier 2007, 234). In other words: when the usual mechanisms of defense (including repression)—which can still master the excessive excitement within the register of the pleasure principle—no longer work, anxiety is brought in as a last resort in order to perform this work of binding, which in this case takes place "beyond the pleasure principle." And the role of the compulsive repetition (of an unpleasant experience) is to give rise to this anxiety. In spite of its unpleasant character, the anxiety is still a defense (against an even bigger displeasure); and the repetition providing this drastic defense is ultimately still in the service of the pleasure principle *qua* lowering of tension—it is a paradoxical extension of the pleasure principle itself. And so, then, is the death drive. If not, one would need to distinguish between the death drive as such, and the *compulsion to repeat* this or that (empirical) traumatic experience. In short, one would need to clearly separate the death drive from repetition. What suggests a move in this last direction in Brassier's work is that he is led to separate the repetition itself from the excess of excitation and to put them, so to speak, on two opposite sides: the excess (or the death drive) is the trace of the aboriginal trauma prior to any experience, and the compulsion to repeat an empirically traumatic experience is a *means* of awakening anxiety in order to master and "bind" the excess. But this would then imply that the (death) drive itself is not intrinsically related to repetition. (Also, it is not quite clear in this account how the aboriginal trauma becomes, appears as, the "unbound excess" [of excitation], which then needs to be bound by anxiety summoned by the repetition of an unpleasant experience.)

These considerations and difficulties could be a good starting point from which to look at the perhaps surprising proximity between Lacan and Deleuze in their readings of Freud on these questions. This proximity goes quite a long way, although at some point their paths clearly diverge: they diverge around the question of a possible "ontology" of the death drive.

DEATH DRIVE II: LACAN AND DELEUZE

The crucial conceptual move shared by Lacan and Deleuze in this matter is a vigorous rejection of the thesis according to which the pleasure principle, conceived as the principle of "lowering tension," constitutes a fundamental, primary principle. Consequently, they also reject the possibility of relating the death drive to a homeostatic tendency ("return to the inanimate"), and hence its subjection—in the last instance—to the pleasure principle as primary.

Although he makes abundant use of the Freudian terms "Eros" (as pleasure) and "Thanatos" (as death drive), Deleuze does not see them as two competing principles, but unambiguously affirms the *primacy of the death drive*: the two are not situated on the same level at all. This affirmation of the death drive may strike us as surprising coming from the allegedly "vitalist" Deleuze, yet there is no ambiguity about it. In the introductory part of *Difference and Repetition*, where he develops one of the most philosophically interesting interpretations of the death drive, he explicitly suggests that the death drive "is the transcendental principle, whereas the pleasure principle is only psychological" (Deleuze 1994, 16).[16] Or: "Eros and Thanatos are distinguished in that Eros must be repeated, can be lived only through repetition, whereas Thanatos (as transcendental principle) is that which gives repetition to Eros" (ibid., 18). In other words, Eros is but part of the logic (of the appearing) of Thanatos or of the death drive, and does not have the status of another, complementary (let alone primary) principle. The death drive is the fundamental (and only) principle, and it has nothing to do with any kind of lowering of tension or "return to nirvana."

Although he does not go in the Kantian direction suggested by Deleuze (positing the death drive as "transcendental"), Lacan argues against the duality of the drives in a very similar way, claiming that "every drive is virtually a death drive" (Lacan 2006c, 719). He also argues against what he takes to be a remainder of Aristotelian metaphysics in Freud. He thus scorns the idea of "backing the primary process up with the principle which, if pleasure were its only claim, would demonstrate nothing, save that we cling to the soul like a tick to a dog's hide. Because what else is the famous lowering of tension with which Freud links pleasure, other than the ethics of Aristotle?" (Lacan 1990, 19).

The idea of the primary principle as that of "lowering tension" is perceived by both Lacan and Deleuze as the heritage of certain philosophical metaphysics, including a "spontaneous metaphysics" of science, to which Freud was not immune, although he was the first to point out things that undermine this spontaneous metaphysics most damagingly. In this precise sense, Lacan's and Deleuze's "modification" of Freud on this point is actually closer to the spirit of Freud himself, to his crucial findings and insights, than the simple acceptance of the claim about an original tendency to lower tension would have been.

But what, then, is the death drive (and its primacy) that Deleuze and Lacan are speaking about? It is certainly not the primacy of some obscure will or tendency to aggression, destruction, death. Deleuze, who embraced the concept of the death drive because of its inherent link with repetition, sees in repetition no less than the very place of original *affirmation*. That is why, for him, the true question is: "How is it that the theme of death, which appears to draw together the most negative elements of psychological life, can be in itself the most positive element, transcendentally positive, to the point of affirming repetition?" (Deleuze 1994, 16). The death drive is decidedly not about destruction and death, it is a complex notion that one needs to think if one wants to posit *affirmation* in terms different from those denounced by Nietzsche as those of an ass saying "yes" (Yea-Yuh) all the time and to everything. For Deleuze, the death drive is a prerogative of true affirmation, insofar as the latter is in itself "*selective*," and is not a simple (and stupid) opposite of negativity. As for Lacan, he relates—in the famous passage from *Seminar XI*, introducing the figure of "lamella"—the death drive to what he calls the "indestructible life" (Lacan 1987, 198). What they both suggest is that the death drive cannot be thought in terms of the simple opposition between life and death, because it is precisely what belies this opposition and (re)configures it in the first place.

The other crucial point shared by Lacan and Deleuze concerns the relation between the erratic "wandering excess" (unbound surplus excitation) and repetition. They both insist that the excess (of excitation) does not exist somewhere independently of (and prior to) repetition, but only and precisely in and through repetition itself. Repetition is not simply a means designed to arouse an anxiety capable of binding the unbound excess (related to the aboriginal trauma). It is also, and paradoxically, that which "produces" or brings about the excess "bound" by anxiety through repetition. The excess of excitation exists only through repetition which strives to bind it, and hence points to a *split at the very heart of repetition itself*. This is probably the most difficult, but also the most important, aspect of their concept of repetition as related to the death drive and to surplus excitation.

In Deleuze's work, this paradox is accounted for by his complex ontology in which repetition itself is two-sided. With every empirical, concrete repetition something else is at stake (and repeated) as well, namely, difference as such, *pure difference*. Repetition does not only repeat something (an "object"), it also repeats difference as such.

Pure difference repeats itself with every individual difference, and it is only through and in relation to this repetition as pure difference that the things exist which we can describe as different, similar, or the same.[17] This is why one should not understand repetition solely in the narrow sense of repeating an identical configuration, but as something no less at work in the colorful variety of differences. The point is that "something" (namely, pure difference) can be repeated in very different forms, while it does not exist somewhere outside and independently of these forms. It has no independent existence, yet at the same time it is not simply reducible to the elements which it repeats. It is their inherent and constitutive difference. Or, in a longer but crucial passage from Deleuze, which also directly relates repetition to the death drive:

Death has nothing to do with a material model. On the contrary, the death instinct may be understood in relation to masks and costumes. Repetition is truly that which disguises itself in constituting itself, that which constitutes itself only by disguising itself. It is not underneath the masks, but is formed from one mask to another, as though from one distinctive point to another, from one privileged instant to another, with and within the variations. The masks do not hide anything except other masks. There is no first term which is repeated.... There is no bare repetition which may be abstracted or inferred from the disguise itself. The same thing is both disguising and disguised. A decisive moment in psychoanalysis occurred when Freud gave up, in certain respects, the hypothesis of real childhood events, which would have played the part of ultimate disguised terms, in order to substitute the power of fantasy which is immersed in the death instinct, where every-thing is already masked and disguised. In short, repetition is in its essence symbolic; symbols or simulacra are the letter of repetition itself. Difference is included in repetition by way of disguise and by the order of the symbol. (Deleuze 1994, 17)

The last part would be the Deleuzian version of the claim made by Brassier: that there is no experienced traumatic *original* of repetition. What is repeated is not some traumatic, and hence repressed, *original* experience. Deleuze pushes this even further by rejecting any kind of causality leading to rep-etition, and positing repetition as an absolute beginning. This leads him to directly reverse the Freudian claim, and to say: "We do not repeat because we repress, we repress because we repeat. Moreover—which amounts to the same thing—we do not disguise because we repress, we repress because we disguise, and we disguise by virtue of the determinant center of repetition" (ibid., 105).[18] The traumatic surplus is produced only *in* and *by* repetition; if anything, repetition (and the excess or surplus object it necessarily intro-duces) is the cause of repression, not the other way around.

In order to unpack these dense speculations, it could be useful to refer back to our earlier discussion of the death drive, and to remember that with it we are also dealing with two splits or two kinds of difference, pertaining to the two sides of the object of the drive.

On the one hand, the object of the drive is different from the object of a need and involves another, surplus satisfaction, following a logic of its own; on the other, this "satisfaction as object" is itself already (or also) a stand-in, a "figure" or "representative" of a faceless negativity. This faceless negativity is none other than the "impossible loss" that could never have registered as loss, the "aboriginal trauma" which is no individual's trauma, but which, in speaking beings, is one with the (originally) missing signifier, the inbuilt loss at stake in the concept of "primary repression," and hence in the concept of the unconscious.

If we relate this to Deleuze (who, not surprisingly, emphatically endorses the notion of "primary repression"),[19] we could say that his concept of the difference which repeats itself with every difference refers precisely to this topology of the drive. Pure difference (as the core of repetition) is this nega-tivity, posited by Deleuze as the most affirmative, productive "force." And we have already seen in earlier chapters how this negativity can be conceived, in psychoanalysis, as a "unifying" singularity: the supposedly originally free and chaotic, fragmented (empirical) multiplicity of the drives is *already a result of* some "unifying" negativity—namely, of the gap around which the drives cir-culate, and which makes drives drives. This fundamental negativity, however, is "unifying" in a very specific sense, which—again—bears some surprising resemblance to the Deleuzian notion of "univocity."

Deleuze has two magisterial concepts with which he thinks the funda-mental negativity at stake here: difference (the radical, individuating differ-ence as conceptualized in *Difference and Repetition*) and the "crack," *fêlure*, which plays a significant role in *The Logic of Sense*. The conceptualization of this uni-fying negativity in terms of the "crack" is less well known and less often dis-cussed, which is all the more reason to recall it in the present context.

Deleuze introduces the concept of the crack (*fêlure*) in relation to F. Scott Fitzgerald's novel *The Crack-Up* (translated in French as *La fêlure*), making a proper concept out of it, and developing it more extensively in his discussion of Zola that concludes— a significant positioning—*The Logic of Sense*. Deleuze takes as his starting point the following extraordinary passage from Zola's *La Bête humaine*:

> The family was really not quite normal, and many of them had some flaw (*fêlure*). At certain times, he could clearly feel this hereditary taint (*fêlure*), not that his health was bad, for it was only nervousness and shame about his attacks that made him lose weight in his early days. But there were attacks of instability in his being, losses of equilibrium like cracks (*cassures*) or holes from which his personality seemed to leak away, amid a sort of thick vapor that deformed everything.[20]

Deleuze first carefully stresses that the crack does not designate the route along which morbid ancestral elements will pass, marking the body. "Hered-ity is not that which passes through the crack, it is the crack itself—*the imper-ceptible rift or the hole*."[21] Heredity does not pass through the crack, it is the crack (the rift or the hole). He further distinguishes this "grand," "epic" heredity from what he calls "small" heredity, which is what we usually mean by this term: the transmission of something determined, transmission as "reproduc-tion" of the same. Although they are in no way reducible to one another, they are very closely related. One way of conceiving this relation would be (again following Zola) in terms of the relation between the crack and its surround-ings. Distributed around the crack are what Zola calls the temperaments, the instincts, the big appetites. Deleuze takes the notion of "instincts" (and their objects) to refer to the corporeal ("empirical") appearance of the crack[22]—a corporeal appearance without which the crack would remain just a "diffuse potentiality." He then proposes the following formulation of the relation between the two levels, which directly echoes the way he describes the relation between repetition (as pure difference/being) and its masks (that which appears) in *Difference and Repetition*, as well as much of Lacan's discussion of the topology of drives:

> If it is true that the instincts are formed and find their object only at the edge of the crack, the crack conversely pursues its course, spreads out its web, changes direction and is actualized in each body in relation to the instincts which open a way for it, sometimes mending it a little, sometimes widening it.... The two orders are tightly joined together, like a ring within a larger ring, but they are never confused.[23]

This, then, is the configuration Deleuze proposes in relation to the two orders or levels involved in the topology of the drives: the crack as faceless negativity that repeats itself with every object of the drive, and constitutes this object (as object) in this very repetition. The crack and the partial object are two different, yet inseparable dimensions of the drive.

The proximity to the Lacanian notion and topology of the drive becomes even more striking in the following passage from *The Logic of Sense*:

> The crack designates, and this emptiness is, Death—the death instinct. The instincts may speak loud, make noise, or swarm, but they are unable to cover up this more profound silence, or hide that from which they come forth and to which they return: the death instinct, *not merely one instinct among others*, but the crack itself around which all the instincts congregate. (Deleuze 1990, 326)

This indeed sounds as if it could come directly from Lacan's *Seminar XI*.[24] The death instinct (death drive) is not one among the drives, but the very crack around which the drives congregate. (This is why Lacan can say that "every drive is virtually a death drive.") Each partial drive (or its object) is a repetition of this crack—a repetition which, in turn, constitutes this object as object.

This is also very interesting in the context of Lacan's discussion of the relationship between sexuality and the (always) partial drives. Sexuality, considered from a phenomenological point of view, appears to be composed of several different partial drives, to which it provides a more or less accomplished unification. (And this was basically Freud's view of the matter.) What we should add to this from the Lacanian perspective—and we are clearly on a speculative level here—is that we could also see sexuation as prior to the partial drives: not as a kind of primary substance, but precisely as the hole/crack around which the drives "congregate" (and in this sense as the Real). I have already pointed out how Lacan emphasizes that there is no sexual ("genital") drive: sexuality (as diverse sexual "activity") appears at the point of its own fundamental lack. Taken at this level, sexuality "unifies" the drives not by uniting them in a more or less coherent whole (of sexual activity), but precisely as the crack around which they circulate and to which they keep returning. The "sexual" refers to the "crack" shared (and repeated) by different drives. Taken at this level, sexuality is indeed synonymous with the death drive, not opposed to it, as Eros is opposed to Thanatos. (And normativity—culturally prescribed normative sexuality—intervenes at the point of this crack; its primary aim is not to unify and "tame" the original heterogeneity of partial drives, but rather to *obfuscate* and at the same time *exploit* this founding crack and its "productivity.")[25] This is also what is usually missed in criticism of the Lacanian take on sexuality and sexual difference: Lacanian psychoanalysis does not promote the (conservative) norm, but exposes the thing that feeds this norm and keeps it in force; this thing is not simply a chaotic multiplicity of the drives, but the "crack in the system." It also maintains that it would be wrong to think that the crack that in-forms human sexuality could simply disappear if we accepted the idea that there is a colorful multiplicity of sexual identities. From the Lacanian perspective, "sexual identity" is a contradiction in terms. The much-criticized psychoanalytic "predilection" for the two (also when it takes the form of the "not-two") comes not from the biology (or anatomy) of sexual reproduction, but from that which, in this reproduction, is missing in biology, *as well as in culture*. Or, in other words, it comes from the fact that copulation is utterly "out of place in human reality, to which it nevertheless provides sustenance with the fantasies by which that reality is constituted" (Lacan 1999, 113).

And—perhaps this is no longer so surprising—when he discusses the "crack," Deleuze also links it to sexuation: as opposed to "*some*" (the somatic cells, the biological cells which form the body of an organism), he writes, "the '*germen*' is the crack—nothing but the crack" (Deleuze 1990, 322). The "germen"—that is to say, the germ cells, the elements involved in sexual reproduction—is the very instance of *fêlure*.

It is of course well known how, in *Difference and Repetition*, Deleuze states emphatically that the motor of repetition is not an impossibility (to repeat); what drives repetition is not a failure, a lack, a deficiency; there is nothing outside it that motivates repetition; repetition itself is both primary "motivator" and motor. Yet we must not understand this Deleuzian stance against "negativity" and "lack" too hastily. As we have seen in his consideration (and appropriation) of the death drive, things are more complicated and more interesting. The point is, rather, that this singular "negativity" (the crack, the hole) is for him the primary site of affirmation. Repetition is the hole/crack that repeats itself, and in doing so it repeats what is around it and related to it. Or, in other words, repetition is negativity taken in the absolute sense: not negativity in relation to something, but original negativity, negativity that is itself productive of what is there and what can be differentiated, compared, said to fail, etc. We could also say that he takes this negativity as such to be the original positive force—as opposed to a secondary notion of negativity (and difference). And the whole question now becomes how to eventually separate this "bad" negativity from a "good" one. It is with this question that some more significant differences between Lacan and Deleuze start to appear.

Before looking into this last point, however, we can already discern another important difference here in relation to Lacan, concerning the concept of negativity and its Deleuzian "translation" into the most positive force.

From the Lacanian perspective, there is something that "motivates" repetition, and this something is precisely an impossibility—although this needs to be understood in a very precise and specific sense. It does not imply, for example, that something is "impossible to be repeated" in its unique singularity; rather, it implies the non-being of what is to be repeated. It is impossible to repeat it because it is not there in the usual sense of the term. This is the Lacanian version of the theory that what is repeated is not an original traumatic experience, interrupting whatever has taken place before, but the interruption itself (which he relates to the Real). And this brings us back to a crucial point in the development of my argument in this book, as well as to the properly psychoanalytic (Lacanian) concept of the "unbound surplus": namely, enjoyment. I have argued that enjoyment appears at the place of the nonexistent ("originally missing") signifier, which—with its very nonexistence—dictates the logic of the signifying chain, "declines it" in a certain way. And it declines it with the help of the enjoyment sticking to (other) signifiers. Enjoyment is the (only) "being," "substance" of that which is ontologically not, of the missing ("originally repressed") signifier. And this enjoyment is the "glue" which, by linking different signifiers in a certain order (of their association), repeats the original negativity. This, I believe, is also what is implied in Brassier's insight according to which "the unbindable excess [is what] makes binding possible" (Brassier 2007, 238),

Certain existing signifying connections (symptoms) or signifying complexes ("formations") are thus not only a disguise under which the original negativity repeats itself, they are also its—more or less fantasmatic, enjoyment-fueled—representations related to the subject of the unconscious. This is to say that—for psychoanalysis—the nexus of representation and enjoyment has to be conceived against the background of an original negativity (call it primal repression, one-less, minus, rift, or crack) as a third element in relation to the unbound excess (enjoyment) and the signifiers. Lacan fortifies this rift, this third, with his concept of the Real (and relates it to the point where a "new signifier" could eventually intervene).

Deleuze, on the other hand, who also starts out from a similar kind of tripartite topology, tends to make it collapse into a double movement of a One. The rift or crack becomes itself the pure movement of the unbound excess appearing with different signifying masks or "disguises."

For psychoanalysis there is thus a difference between the fundamental negativity (a "minus") and the excessive surplus (-enjoyment) that emerges at its place, and repeats the original negativity by linking, "gluing," the signifiers with which this negativity appears in *a certain order*. For Deleuze, however, the excess/surplus is *directly* the pure productive excess of negativity (crack, Difference) repeating itself in different disguises and with different signifiers or symbols. The original negativity directly *is* the "positive," "productive" movement or force ("drive"). This is also what the "plane of immanence" basically refers to: "The same thing is both disguising and disguised." What disappears here—to repeat—is precisely the difference between the original negativity and the surplus that emerges at its place and binds the signifiers in a certain order (which necessarily depends upon contingencies of individual history).

In what Deleuze will call "realized ontology," all that remains is the Difference itself (pure difference, not a difference between this and that). This Difference is pure being *qua* being in its univocity. And it equals pure *movement*, just as the fêlure, the "crack," is finally not so much a rift as a pure movement or force. This shift from *topological* to *dynamic* tropes is indeed crucial for Deleuze: the topological non-coincidence of being and appearing, their rift, is "liquefied" into Being as a pure *movement* of Difference.

By "liquefying" the difference (non-coincidence) of being and appearing into a pure differentiating movement of Being itself, Deleuze obliterates the Real that keeps repeating itself in this difference. This, at least, would be the Lacanian stance. With the notion of the Real, Lacan gives conceptual support to the rift, the crack, implied by yet invisible in the deployment of differences, and repeated with them. He extracts it from its invisibility, claiming that psychoanalysis is in a position to give it some minimal consistency.

Whereas Deleuze moves to ontologize this Real, and makes it the real Being *qua* being, it is essential for Lacan to keep them apart. This Lacanian holding apart of Being and the Real does not imply that Being is not real— the Real is precisely not a predicate. Lacan's reservations about something like psychoanalytic ontology is well known. He has no wish to develop his own ontology. Yet the reason does not, perhaps, lie in his conviction that ontology is meaningless (after the transcendental turn) and necessarily "metaphysical"; on the contrary. If there is one person who has always refused to consider psychoanalysis as exempt from ontological interrogation, it is Lacan. His point is, rather, that the very notion of ontology (as "the science of being *qua* being") has to be expanded by an additional concept (the Real) that holds and marks the place of its inherent contradiction/impossibility. And the subject is the effect of this contradiction, not an offshoot of being. There is the subject because there is the Real.

This is where Lacan and Deleuze seem to be furthest apart: whereas for Deleuze "realism" implies radical desubjectivation, for Lacan (the effect of) subjectivation is the very instance (or "proof") of an irreducible Real.

In this respect it is no coincidence that in the so-called "new materialisms," many of which are based upon Deleuzian foundations,[26] the main philosophical front (the main battlefield) usually lies along the line of the question of the subject. Most of the conceptual propositions related to new materialisms aim both at "getting out of the subject" (the supposed discursive or transcendental cage) and at "getting the subject out" (of the landscape of new ontologies)—or, at least, ascribing it to a not particularly significant local point of this landscape.

The question I would like to raise here is simply this: Can there be serious materialism without the subject—that is, without a strong concept of the subject, such as we find, for example, in Lacan? And—in passing—it is significant that even though new materialisms usually take their starting point in rejecting the so-called "linguistic turn," and all that is labeled "structuralism" and "poststructuralism," they actually share with them precisely this conviction according to which the "subject" is a rotten apple in the barrel of philosophical concepts. One reason why Lacan stands out in the context of (post) structuralism is precisely because he does not subscribe to this view. To put it very simply: if language, discourse, or structure were consistent ontological categories, there would be no subject.

But in order to work our way up to these questions, let me start at a simpler point. One of the definitions and images of materialism (as realism) is as follows: contrary to deceptive and groundless ideals and idealizations, materialism exposes the brute reality, reality without embellishments, the material truth or basis of things that seem to stand on their own. Let me borrow an example from Žižek: the following quote from Marcus Aurelius's *Meditations*:

> Like seeing roasted meat and other dishes in front of you and suddenly realizing: This is a dead fish. A dead bird. A dead pig. Or that this noble vintage is grape juice, and the purple robes are sheep wool dyed with shellfish blood. Or making love—something rubbing against your penis, a brief seizure and a little cloudy liquid.
>
> Perceptions like that—latching onto things and piercing through them, so we see what they really are. That's what we need to do all the time—all through our lives when things lay claim to our trust—to lay them bare and see how pointless they are, to strip away the legend that encrusts them.[27]

Materialism would thus mean, in this account: the reality minus the illusion which accompanies it and keeps transforming it into something quite different. The maneuver described by Marcus Aurelius aims at bursting the bubble of the imaginary, and forcing us to face reality such as it is. Žižek adds another example of this strategy, which was supposed to guard (Catholic) men against sins of the flesh: when you are tempted by a voluptuous female body, imagine what it will look like in a couple of decades or, better still, imagine what lurks even now beneath the skin: the raw flesh and bones, bodily fluids, half-digested food and excrement....

In other words, in the pair of the sublime and the gruesome body, the materialist perspective is supposed to be on the side of the gruesome body: the sobering perspective revealing, behind a beautiful and deceptive appearance, the ugly material Real....To the way Žižek convincingly dismantles this perspective I would like to add another possible path toward the same problem: the sheer terms of the description (sublime versus gruesome) already point to a problem at the heart of this conception. We can expose it in two steps.

(1)   What is supposed to be the sobering effect of realist materialism points in fact to a crack/gap in this realism itself. Reality "such as it is" (without embellishments) appears in all these configurations—directly or indirectly—as ugly, gruesome. In other words: in order for it to "sober us up" (wake us from the illusion), it has to be perceived as *more* than it is: it has to be invested with a series of quite subjective affects—repugnance, aversion, and the like. In order to get to reality "such as it is," a (subjective) *surplus* is needed (or produced), a surplus or excess which is precisely not reducible to "reality such as it is." (The fact that rotting flesh incites affects of disgust, or at least extinguishes our desire immediately, is no less mediated by the window of [our] fantasy than what appears as sublime.)

(2)   Yet—and this is the second step—this is not to say that contrary to naïve materialism, which strives to discover the naked material reality of things in themselves (but never quite succeeds), we are simply defending the inaccessibility of a thing in itself and its necessary *mediation* by the subjective, which has "always-already" taken place. Rather, what is at stake, and what one could argue for, is a different kind of materialism which is precisely not based on the opposition between "naked" reality, stripped of all subjective illusions and investments (reality such as it exists independently of the subject), and an "always-already" subjective/subjectivized (or subject-constituted) reality. For this opposition is false or, better, it is not genuinely "materialist." It is only by working through this excess

(and by following its distortions through) that we get to the thing in itself, for this thing in itself is already contradictory.

The thesis, in its simplest form, would be that we should consider the following possibility: if reality appears with an irreducible excess "over" itself, then this excess (or non-coincidence with itself) is not simply or only a subjective distortion, but should also be seen as indicative of a split or contradiction in this reality itself. How can this claim be made in any convincing way? Precisely by arguing for a specific concept of the subject, which starts from shifting the ground of the discussion from the question of affirming or denying the existence of reality independent of the subject, to a different kind of perspective which affirms, and combines, the following two propositions: (1) there is indeed a reality that exists independently of the subject (that is independent of subjective mediation or constitution); (2) the subject (the structure of subjectivity in the strong sense of the term, in its very excessiveness) is precisely that which gives us access to reality independent of the subject.

If we simply remove the subject and its distortions/excessiveness, we may indeed get a "neutral reality"; actually, we cannot get *anything but* some form of neutrality, and this is where the problem lies. For what if reality is not neutral, but torn by an inherent impossibility and contradiction? Or, more precisely, what if neutrality itself is not "neutral," but already implies a subjective imposition, a normative "neutralization"? In that case the subjective excessiveness brings us closer to the truth, as well as to the possibility of engaging with reality's contradictions.

This is the problem of the realism which operates with the notion of reality such as it is "independently of ourselves." The problem is not simply that we can never exempt ourselves from the reality of which we are part, and that we cannot reflexively subtract our distortion and in this way obtain a pure, independent reality. The problem is deeper and much more fundamental: reality as it is independently of ourselves appears (comes into view) only "dependently on us" *as subjects*—not in the sense of being caused or constituted by us, but in the sense that reality's own inherent negativity/contradiction appears as part of this reality precisely in the form of the subject. (Apart from other things,) the subject is an *objective* embodiment of reality's contradiction. This, I think, would be the gist of Lacan's materialism: of course I am determined, as a subject, by things that exist independently of me; yet the subjective position, or subjectivation, is not only a concrete and singular way in which things determine me, it is also and at the same time the subjectivation of a paradox/contradiction involved in the very things that determine me (this paradox/contradiction exists "in itself" only as this objectivation-subjectivation, or objectivation via the subject).

What this implies could be formulated as follows: we get to certain aspects of objective reality only by insisting on the irreducibility of the subject. And not, for example, by a hasty, precipitate objectivation of the subject itself, as we find, for example, in the materialism involved in some versions of object-oriented ontology, positing that the subject is simply just another object—an object among other objects, with its own specific characteristics.[28] If the subject were simply one object among others, there would be no need for the concept of the subject (in the strong philosophical and psychoanalytic sense); the term "person" (or "human being") would suffice. The subject names an object that is precisely not just an object among others—this is the whole point, and there is no need for this statement to provoke in us an immediate attack of self-limiting modesty, inciting us to write on banners: "Down with the privileges of the subject! Down with its exceptional status!" For in doing this we are jeopardizing—among many other things—precisely that political dimension of ontology that inspires this kind of democratic and egalitarian project.

The stronger thesis that I propose to defend is thus as follows: the subject is not simply an object among many objects, it is also the form of existence of the contradiction, antagonism, at work in the very existence of objects as objects. It refers to the way in which the impasse/contradiction of reality in which different objects appear exists within this same reality. The subject exists among objects, yet it exists there as the point that gives access to a possible objectivation of their inner antagonism, its inscription into their reality. In this precise sense, the fine-sounding thesis about the "democracy of objects" (all objects are ontologically the same, and all are equally worthy of our attention) could be seen as actually (and quite "subjectively") obfuscating reality "such as it is": antagonistic. The subject modestly, humbly, retreats to one, not particularly distinguished place in infinite reality, and thus efficiently masks its split, producing reality as neutral and non-problematic in itself (or at least untouchable in its problematic character). Contrary to this, one can conceive of the subject as an existence/form of a certain difficulty (the Real), and as a "response" to it. This response can well be subjective/pathological, but it is never completely reducible to its own pathology; it also carries with it the Real (of a possibly universal bearing) that is not accessible—in itself—in any way but via the very figure of the subject. This is why, by (im)modestly positing the subject as a more or less insignificant point in the universe, one deprives oneself of the possibility to think, radically and seriously, the very "injustice" (asymmetry, contradiction) that made one want to develop an egalitarian ontological project in the first place.

The (Lacanian) subject is not simply the one who thinks, it is also and above all what makes certain contradictions accessible to thought; it is the way in which these contradictions appear as a "matter of thought." And without this particular "matter of thought" it is difficult to speak of *materialism*. Another way of putting this would be: Lacan's gesture, which is often misread as his version of "correlationism," consists in introducing a short circuit of the epistemological and ontological levels (of knowledge and being) in the form of their joint/common negativity (lack of knowledge falls into a lack of being)—and the concept of the subject (as subject of the unconscious) is situated at this precise juncture.

This is why, for example—and this is crucial—if we cannot think something without a contradiction, we should not take a step back from this impossibility (recognizing and accepting it as impossibility, or inaccessibility to thought); instead, and on the contrary, we have to take this contradiction and impossibility *as the very Real which IS accessible to thought*. I have already stressed how logical paradoxes, impasses of formalization, *are* the points where thought thinks the Real; this was one of Lacan's strongest convictions. To think a paradox or contradiction does not mean to stare at it with fascination, as in a kind of mystical revelation of the Absolute; it means precisely what it says—to *think* it.

So perhaps this would be a good formulation of materialism: materialism is thinking which advances as thinking of contradictions.[29] And this is what makes psychoanalysis a materialist theory (and practice): it starts by thinking a problem/difficulty/contradiction, not by trying to think the world such as it is independently of the subject.

After this excursion into the question of the subject, let us return to our prior discussion of what separates Lacan and Deleuze at the very peak of their proximity. In relation to the central question of repetition, they both share a basic conceptual matrix according to which what repeats itself could be formulated by the term "One-plus": something (some discernible entity) plus the surplus that invests and drives it. Deleuze directly identifies the *plus* with the movement of absolute difference, and hence with the real of being. This is the origin of the fundamental Deleuzian duality and its (simple) reversal, accomplished by repetition. In graphic terms: the repetition of the One-plus, driven by the "plus," has to eventually differentiate—with the help of its centrifugal force—precisely between these two terms ("One" and "plus"); it has to break their link and throw out the One of some hypostasized being (or some particular difference, and hence identity) to the benefit of Being (or Difference) as singularity of a pure movement. In this way the repetition, so to speak, "purges *itself*," separates itself from its weighty encumbrance. This, for example, is how Deleuze reads the Nietzschean eternal return: "The wheel in the eternal return is at once both production of repetition on the basis of difference and selection of difference on the basis of repetition" (Deleuze 1994, 42). Taking into account the link between repetition and difference, we could say that what is at stake here is the repetition as inner differentiation (or "purge") of the Difference. What does this mean? What is repeated comes from the pure negativity of difference which, in repetition, is always-already something (that is to say, some entity which comes under the categories of analogy, similarity, identity); at the same time, this repetition itself is a "centrifugal *force*" that expels all that which, of the difference, gets "reified" into something in this same repetition (ibid., 297). That is to say: it expels all that comes under the categories of analogy, similarity, identity.

The centrifugal force of repetition in its most radical form thus not only introduces the difference at the very core of repetition, but also "realizes" this difference—it realizes it by extracting repetition itself from repetition, by extracting what is *new* from the mechanism of repetition that produced it. This is what could be described, in Deleuze's terms, as concept-project, the latter being no less than the project of *realized ontology*: "However, the only realized Ontology—in other words, the univocity of being—is repetition" (Deleuze 1994, 303). Difference is the only and the original being, yet at the same time it (still) needs to be realized, that is to say, *repeated* and thus separated from all the metaphysical and dialectical encumbrance that constitutes the history of Being and of its thought. This task can be accomplished by the "centrifugal force" of the repetition itself, which will thus bring about the separation between what I referred to above as "good" and "bad" negativity. And the triumph of "good"—that is, of the whole series of the Deleuzian positive predicates (horizontally rhizomatic versus vertically hierarchical, negativity as positive excess versus negativity as lack, multiplicity versus one, nomadic versus static, different versus similar or identical, exceptional versus ordinary...)—is, so to speak, inscribed in the force of repetition itself. That is why "realized ontology" looks very much like a *political project* or, more precisely, like something that can do without politics, since it hands its task over to ontology.

Several decades ago, the decline of politics proper (and of conceiving politics as effective thought) was accompanied by the rise of "ethics." The (philosophical and social) success of ethics was linked to its promise to carry out the task of politics better than politics. This is how the rising ethical discourse presented itself: the new ethics to replace the old politics. Concepts like "antagonism," "class struggle," "emancipation," and "politics" itself were generally replaced by notions of "tolerance," "recognition of the Other," and by the self-imposed rules of political correctness.[30] Ever since the beginning of the last economic and political crisis, starting in the early 2000s, the limits of this "ethics as politics" were becoming more salient, and the notion of politics as politics started reentering the stage. At the same time, we were (and still are) witnessing an astounding rise of so-called new ontologies and new materialisms (to a large extent, albeit not exclusively, inspired by Deleuze), which paradoxically advance by making a very similar kind of promise to the one ethics made a while ago: to be able to carry out the task of politics better than politics. The massive use (and popularity) of the word "ontology" is symptomatic in this respect. And so are many terms that describe these new ontologies; "democracy of objects" is just one of them.

How, then, is Lacan's conceptual (and "practical") maneuver different? Where Deleuze speaks about *selection* of difference based on repetition, Lacan speaks about the *production* of a new signifier that puts an end to repetition. Although they both emphasize a "selection," that is, a *separation* concerning something at the very heart of the repetition/difference itself, the crucial divergence lies in the way in which this separation takes place, as well as in the nature of what it produces (as its novelty).What, for Lacan, can bring about the separation within the repeating entity (of One-plus) is not the centrifugal-selective force of the repetition itself; this separation is possible only through a third term, produced in the course of analysis: S_1, a *new signifier* (situated at the place of "production" in the analytic discourse). This signifier is a new kind of One—a One that differs from the One which is repeated (in neurosis or in everyday life). The One that is repeated is a One-plus, a compound of a signifier and enjoyment. Here we are at the level of the signifying chain and its inherent peripeteias. The expression "signifying chain" refers to the fact that a signifier is never alone, but is *virtually* connected—via the lack that constitutes it (the One-less)—with all other signifiers, and *actually* connected to those in which surplus-enjoyment has realized ("glued") this connection through repetition. For it is precisely this surplus that binds, connects different Ones (signifiers) in concrete circumstances. Analysis, on the other hand, leads to the production of a different, self-standing One: to *One as one alone*.

> The One at stake in the S_1 which the subject produces, so to say, at the ideal point of analysis, is, differently from the One at stake in repetition, the One as One alone [Un seul]. It is the One so far as, whatever the difference that exists, of all the differences that exist and that all have the same value, there is only one, and that is the difference. (Lacan 2011, 165)

This also refers to another significant concept elaborated in some detail by Lacan in this same seminar (... ou pire); namely, what he writes as Il y a de l'Un (which he further abbreviates as Y a de l'Un, and even Yad'lun): "there's (some) One," with the French partitive article de paradoxically suggesting an unspecified quantity of One. This term is designed by Lacan to include in the notion of the (countable) One what is usually excluded from it, namely, the pure difference out of which and with which it emerges. This pure difference (or "hole," trou) is, he suggests, the "foundation of the One." This foundation can be conceived as an "entrance door designated from the lack, from the place where there is a hole. If you want a picture, I would gladly represent the foundation of this *Yad'lun* as a sack. One cannot exist except in the figure of a sack, a sack with a hole. Nothing is One which doesn't come from this sack, or go into it. Taken intuitively, this is the original foundation of One" (Lacan 2011, 147).

And the new kind of One (S_1), in its singularity, is very closely related to this foundational "hole." Its function is to give a signifying support to the rift, the crack, implied by yet invisible in the deployment of differences (symptoms), and repeated with them. This is also the way in which the seemingly abstract notion of *Y a de l'Un* (abbreviated into *Yad'lun*) is related to analytic practice. Lacan indicates this relation (or perhaps we should say this coincidence) with the homonymy "*y'a d'l'inconscient*" ("there is the unconscious").[31] The Freudian/Lacanian concept of the unconscious is thus directly related to the notion of *Yad'lun* (and to the Real implied by it). The unconscious is not a *realm* of being; the unconscious "exists" because there is a crack in being out of which comes whatever discursive (ontological) consistency there is. And the production of a new signifier puts us at the point of this "beginning"— which is not a beginning in time, but a beginning as a point in the structure where things are being generated. The new signifier is supposed to name the difference that makes all the difference(s).

It is crucial to note that in the quote from Lacan above, the emphasis is on production: what is at stake is not that in the course of analysis one *finds* the missing signifier—the latter is precisely not something that could be found, dug up from the unconscious. For it is most literally not there (and this is *why* there is the unconscious—the unconscious *is* the crack implied by the one-less). This is not a repressed signifier, but a signifier whose non-being is the only thing that makes repression possible, and structurally precedes it. (This is where Freud introduced the hypothesis of "primal repression.") The new signifier, S_1, does not replace this "hole" with which the signifying order appears, it does not close it or do away with it; rather, it produces it (by producing its letter) as something that can work as an emancipatory weapon. In what sense?

> Briefly put, the operation of the analytic discourse consists in making a model of neurosis. Why? Because this robs it of the dose of enjoyment. This enjoyment does not demand any privilege; there is only one way to do it for everybody. All reduplication kills it. It survives only so far as its repetition is hollow [*vaine*], that is to say, always the same. And it is the introduction of the model that ends [*achève*] this hollow repetition. The achieved [*achevée*] repetition dissolves it, since it is a simplified repetition. (Lacan 2011, 151–152)

The model of neurosis succeeds in repeating its enjoyment, hence killing it off. However, if this is the ideal end of analysis, its beginning very much relies on enjoyment, and on putting it to work—it is only and precisely its work that eventually produces the "new signifier." For we must ask: what is it that makes possible the construction of the "model" of neurosis to begin with, and ends in the production of a new signifier? This is certainly not the analyst's knowledge, her expertise, but has to come from the subject herself. And, as a matter of fact, Lacan is most explicit on this point: the new signifier "is produced from the placing of the subject at the level of enjoyment in talking" (Lacan 2011, 165). This, of course, is another way of saying that it is produced "starting from the efflorescence of the signifier," its polysemic babble, its equivocities (ibid., 151).

Enjoyment is thus the very means of production of the signifier that eventually kills it off; this signifier interposes itself between the (signifying) enjoyment and the hole/gap at the place of which the latter appears, "takes place."

This, then, is an important conceptual feature that separates Lacan from Deleuze: the surplus ("the erratic/unbound excess," enjoyment) is not in itself the real scene of emancipation, but the means of production of that which eventually realizes this "emancipation"; the eventual tectonic shift does not take place at the level of this surplus, but thanks to the newly produced signifier. It is the signifier of the "hole" at the place of which enjoyment appears that repeats this "hole" in different disguises or signifying formations. This new signifier depends on the subject's individual and contingent history, yet it is not simply part of this history. It is what reiteration, repetition of this history in analysis, produces as a word that works. Works at what? At shifting something in our relation to the signifying order that (in)forms our being. As early as 1957, in his essay "The Instance of the Letter in the Unconscious"—and this title chimes strongly with what we are developing here—Lacan writes:

> It is by touching, however lightly, on man's relation to the signifier—in this case, by changing the procedures of exegesis—that one changes the course of his history by modifying the moorings of his being. (Lacan 2006c, 438)

This, then, would be the more complex schema: the placing of the subject at the level of enjoyment in talking enables the production of the new signifier from the perspective of which it is now possible to effect a separation at the heart of the One-plus involved in repetition. This new signifier is the event proper, and it triggers a new subjectivation.

The new signifier is the algorithm that disorients the drive by cutting off the well-established routes of its satisfaction. It is what inserts itself at the very core of the double face of the drive and of its "satisfaction." In itself, the drive is quite indiscriminate, indifferent toward what it satisfies along the path of pursuing its one and only goal, which is simply to "return into circuit" (Lacan 1987, 179), that is, to repeat itself, as Deleuze reads this. This is the "affirmative" force of repetition (repetition for the sake of repetition) related to the drive: not something that failed, but repetition itself as the sole "drive" of the drive. The drive is always satisfied. However, in its very indifference it is also always supportive of whatever complicated paths and extraordinary objects our enjoyment may choose *under the sign of repression*. It doesn't care one way or the other. By itself, the drive does not work against repression (which retroactively works on repetition). In this precise sense the death drive is as much an accomplice of repression as it is utterly indifferent to it. This also means that one cannot simply count on it to make the "right" selection (which is what is implied in the Nietzschean/Deleuzian perspective). There is absolutely no guarantee that, left to itself, the death drive will expel the right (that is, the wrong) things, as Deleuze seems to maintain. One needs something else, or more: only a new signifier (and the new *subjectivation* triggered by it) can effect and sustain the separation at the very heart of the drive. Not a *force* (be it centrifugal or other), only a *letter* can disentangle what exists only in entangled form, and hence eventually change this form itself.

BEING, EVENT, AND ITS CONSEQUENCES: LACAN AND BADIOU

This is also and precisely the point where what we can call "Lacanian politics" comes in. Or, perhaps more precisely, this is where the space of politics opens up. This space is essentially connected to the gap/crack of the unconscious—not a specific unconscious, but the unconscious as the concept of the gap with which discursive reality appears, and struggles. Politics, in the strong sense of the term, always involves a reactivation of this gap. It is clear, at least, that this is how Lacan conceives the politics of psychoanalysis. For this is the point he makes in his own quarrel with the turn psychoanalysis has taken since Freud:

> In actual fact, this dimension of the unconscious that I am evoking *has been forgotten*, as Freud had quite clearly foreseen. The unconscious has closed itself up against his message thanks to those active practitioners of orthopaedics that the analysts of the second and third generation became, busying themselves, by psychologising analytic theory, in stitching up this gap. (Lacan 1987, 23)

But what are the implications of this outside the configuration of the analytic cure; that is to say, what are its more general political implications? Some see the concept of a "new signifier" as leading to the question of a new kind of (political) organization, which is certainly an interesting path to pursue. And one needs to pursue it "beyond" Lacan, insofar as the organization of the psychoanalytic community is not usually considered to be Lacan's strong point.[32]

There are also some very interesting connections (as well as differences) between Lacan and Badiou on these questions, which have their own political implications. Let us briefly run through them. For one thing, it is quite clear that the Lacanian notion of the Real has a great deal in common with the Badiouian notion of the Event—starting with its relation to being and ontology. We have already emphasized how crucial it is for Lacan to keep the notions of being and of the Real apart. Let us recapitulate: Lacan conceives of the Real as the point of the internal impossibility/contradiction of being, which is why he holds the Real to be the bone in the throat of every ontology: in order to speak of "being *qua* being," one has to amputate something in being that is not being. That is to say, the Real is that which ontology has to cut off in order to be able to speak of "being *qua* being." And this is almost exactly how Badiou situates the Event: ontology "prohibits" the Event, "the [mathematical/ontological] axiom of foundation de-limits being by the prohibition of the event" (Badiou 2005, 190); "the event belongs to that-which-is-not-being-*qua*-being" (ibid., 189). Furthermore, like the Lacanian Real, the Event in Badiou is not related to the pure empirical nature of what-happens, but belongs to conceptual *construction* (ibid., 178). Then there is the notion of the "ultra one," which is crucial in this construction, and implies the conceptual distinction of an Event from its site "by the interposition of itself between the void and itself" (ibid., 182). Is this not almost exactly how Lacan characterizes the new "new signifier" in its singularity—the "one alone" that interposes itself between the void/hole and what occurs at its place? There is also the importance of "*interpretative intervention,*" which alone can "declare that an event is presented in a situation" (ibid., 181). These similarities are by no means superficial; there is a firm (and shared) logic that supports them and links Badiou to Lacan. At the same time, there is also something like an inaugural *décalage,* a shifting of terms that accounts for the subsequent differences between Lacan and Badiou.

To put it very simply: for Badiou, the prohibition of the Event is the "consequence of a law of the discourse on being-*qua*-being" (Badiou 2005, 190). For Lacan, the law of the discourse on being-*qua*-being is itself a consequence of an impossibility (gap) with which it occurs. It could be said that for Lacan all being is discursive, but at the same time the discursive is not-all. And this is precisely why being (as discursive) is inseparable from its own "impossibility." In other terms, what is at stake here is, first, an impossibility that pertains to being, and not (only) to the Event.

Lacan's claim here is in fact stronger than Badiou's: it is not simply that the *discourse* on being-*qua*-being necessarily prohibits something; it is that being as such is inseparable from its own impossibility, since there is no being outside the discourse, yet the discourse itself is strictly coextensive with a gap. Let us recall:

> Discourse begins from the fact that here there is a gap....But, after all, nothing prevents us from saying that it is because discourse begins that the gap is produced. It is a matter of complete indifference toward the result. What is certain is that discourse is implied in the gap. (Lacan 2006b, 107)

Badiou's ontology, on the other hand, is based upon the thesis according to which being-qua-being is but pure inconsistent multiplicity.—That is to say, not a multiplicity of ones, but a multiplicity that is always a multiplicity of multiplicity (of multiplicity...), so that the eventual point when this stops cannot be "one," but can only be the void. The discursive comes in only as a presentation of this multiplicity, involving a "count-as-one". For Badiou, the "count-as-one" is the condition of any thinkable situation or thing: whereas the purely multiple is inconsistent, and is a pure "excess beyond itself," all consistent thought supposes a structure, a count-as-one, such that every presented or presentable multiple is consistent. In this respect, the count-as-one (and with it the notion of "one") is perfectly compatible with the notion of pure multiplicity. However, excess beyond itself, which is the very being of Being as purely multiple, also takes place on the level of what is already counted-for-one, that is, on the level of presentation, within a set, or within what Badiou calls a "situation" (which is another word for "set"): it takes place as the excess of the parts of a given multiple or set over its elements.[33] This excess, which Badiou also calls l'excès errant, the "wandering excess," is one of the crucial notions of his ontology, for he holds "the wandering [errance] of the excess to be the real of being" (Badiou 1999, 81).

And this brings us to what I believe is the core of the difference between Lacan and Badiou, which concerns precisely the status of this excess or surplus.

For Badiou, the uncountable excess of the multiple beyond itself, which thus escapes representation, is no less than the real of being, the "being of Being." Badiou perceives the "wandering excess" as strictly coextensive with the multiple; being-qua-being is the inconsistent multiple (of the multiple), which is as such pure excess beyond itself. The excess is thus an immediate implication of the multiple. Even though Badiou emphasizes that this multiple is ultimately a multiple of a "void" (and not of some atomic elements), this void does not amount to negativity in any strong meaning of the word; all it suggests is a desubstantialization of being. We thus have multiplicity, the multiple as positivity of excess in the absence of all primary substance—and it seems that in this respect Badiou actually comes surprisingly close to Deleuze. Lacan, on the other hand, insists on a different theme, which could be formulated as follows: the *"wandering excess" is not the implication of the multiple (multiplicity), but of the One-less, of the minus-one.* The elusive, uncountable, yet irreducible excess is the other side—not of One, but of the "minus one" as the ontological foundation of (any countable) one. The excess exists, flourishes at the structural place of the *minus one*, and here it proliferates as its irreducible material plus.

This is precisely why, for Lacan, the wandering excess cannot be the *Real* of being, but is its *symptom*. And unlike a symptom, which exists, although it lacks adequate representation, the Real of being is not something that exists, yet does not count, but rather something which does not exist at the level of being, yet something we can reconstruct (from the symptoms), formalize as its Real. For Lacan, the Real of being can only be the letter of the constitutive deadlock of being. In this context one should perhaps not yield too quickly to the explanatory charm of certain politically very significant examples given by Badiou: for example, the *sans-papiers* as a contemporary political instance of the wandering excess. For Badiou this is an example of being which obviously exists, yet has no symbolic status, which is why it can be treated, at the level of the state and its mode of representation, as if it did not exist. It is an unrepresented (uncountable) excess of the state-multiple beyond itself. The difference with Lacan in this respect is of course not that for Lacan something like the *sans-papiers* would not count as a critical problem; it resides in the formulation of what exactly is the problem here (where it lies), and hinges on the distinction between the symptom and the Real. To state it briefly: a symptom is a formation of being, whereas the Real is its deadlock (non-being) which this formation keeps repeating. The Real does not present/represent itself, what it does is that—as the inherent deadlock, "minus," of being—it dictates and directs the processes of the (re)presentation of being. In this sense, the *sans-papiers* (as the figure of the wandering excess) are not the Real of being, but, so to speak, the "casualties" of the Real of being. They are the symptom as material embodiment of a fundamental deadlock (of a given whole), a deadlock which does not exist somewhere outside and independently of this embodiment, yet is not directly identical with it either. This is why if, for Lacan, the identification with a symptom is possible, there is no possible identification with the Real—where there is, strictly speaking, nothing to identify with. This way of conceptualizing things not only resists, but also efficiently blocks the possibility of (political, artistic, or love-related) romanticism of the Real, which actually lies at the very basis of what Badiou recognizes as the antiphilosophical "suture" of philosophy, its abandoning itself to one of its conditions. There is nothing beautiful, sublime, or authentic about the Real. Nothing gets "revealed" with the Real. The Real is the place of the "systemic violence" that exists and repeats itself in the form of the "unbound excess." The emphasis on the concept of the Real, as well as the imperative that we must formalize it, are not Lacan's ways of celebrating it, they are means of locating and formulating the problems of the (discursive) structure.

In the concluding part of *Being and Event*, Badiou suggests that the only important difference between Lacan and himself finally "bears upon the localization of the void" (Badiou 2005, 432). Whereas he, Badiou, reserves the proper name of void-set for being-*qua*-being, Lacan reserves it for the subject. This (which Badiou reads as an essentially Cartesian gesture) leaves the subject in an "excentred dependency with regards to language," which is precisely what Badiou wants to avoid. Against the concept of the subject as an effect of language (or of the signifier), and hence as "identifiable within the uniform networks of experience," Badiou wants to assert "the rarity of the subject, which suspends its occurrence from the event, from the intervention, and from the generic paths of fidelity" (ibid., 432).

However, is this really where the core of the difference between Lacan and Badiou is to be situated? As our previous discussion implies, this difference relates not simply to what one or the other chose as the proper name of the void, but to the status of negativity: Badiou has no strong concept of negativity at the level of being. Being deploys itself as pure excess over itself. For Lacan, on the other hand, the pure excess of being is already a result of a minus-one, of the gap that appears together with discourse. So when Lacan says that the subject is "an effect that is what is presumed as such by a functioning of the signifier," this does not simply mean that the subject is an effect of language. It means that subject is the proper name of that in language which is not, of the gap in it. The subject (of the unconscious) is not simply the name of a void-set, it is the name of the *gap* pertaining to discourse, as well as the name of the *effect* that takes place *because* there is this gap in discourse. In this precise sense we can say that for Lacan the subject is both "identifiable within the uniform networks of experience" (that is, fairly common, presumed by the functioning of the signifier), *and rare*—that is, emerging only from time to time. Psychoanalytic examples of the latter—that is, of sudden and *surprising*, unexpected emergences of the subject—range from slips of the tongue, dreams, jokes, to shattering love encounters. It is important to see how the subject emerging here is not simply an effect of language, but of its breaking down, of its discontinuity. This is why Lacan will insist—and this is crucial:

Following the thread of analytic discourse goes in the direction of nothing less than breaking up anew (*rebriser*), inflecting, marking with its own camber—a camber that could not even be sustained as that of lines of force— that which produces the break (*faille*) or discontinuity. Our recourse, in language (*lalangue*), is that which shatters it (*la brise*). (Lacan 1999, 44)

The slight (yet also consequential) difference between Badiou and Lacan could thus be formulated as follows: for Badiou, pure being is inconsistent, but it is all fully there, so to speak. Being as such is not ridden with any impossibility. The latter only pertains to, or originates in, its (re)presentation, and leads to the theory of the Event and its ontological impossibility or prohibition. What follows from Lacan's conceptualizations, on the other hand, is that the two are related: an Event is possible (can happen) because of the impossibility inherent to being.

This difference also explains why it never occurs to Badiou to relate his notion of the "wandering excess" to the psychoanalytic notion of the "unbound surplus," that is, to enjoyment as always *surplus*-enjoyment/excitation. It is indeed striking how Badiou, who is otherwise a most incisive reader of Freud and Lacan, mostly uses the notion of enjoyment in an entirely non- or pre-analytic sense—as an individual hedonistic idiosyncrasy, devoid of any possible bearing at the level of truth. That is to say: he takes it to be something titillating, but at the same time completely irrelevant. For Lacan, on the other hand, enjoyment is, rather, tiresomely monotonous, yet by no means irrelevant: it takes place at the precise point where something is lacking in the discursive, and "cambers" the discursive structuring with its repetition. This is why the analyst has to allow this enjoyment to speak and have patience with its tiresome, repetitious, monotonous work, from session to session, listening to stories that seem unique, titillating and exciting only to the subjects recounting them. Yet the analyst must listen very carefully, since from time to time this recounting posits a word at the right place—a place in the construction of a "new signifier." ...

This may come as a surprise, but with the claims presented above Lacan actually reiterates some of his early claims, like this one in *Seminar II*: "Desire is a relation of being to lack. This lack is the lack of being properly speaking. It isn't the lack of this or that, but lack of being whereby (*par quoi*) being exists." And, a bit further on: "If being were only what it is, there wouldn't even be room to talk about it. Being comes into existence as an exact function of this lack" (Lacan 1988, 223). The idea that being is generated out of its own "lack of being" is already here. However, these are early considerations, and Lacan does not simply return to them in his late seminars, but reaffirms them within what is now a more complex, elaborated conceptual edifice. This is how he formulates the new emphasis: "What we must get used to is substituting the 'para-being' (*par-être*)—the being 'para,' being beside—for the being that would take flight" (Lacan 1990, 44).

"The being that would take flight" is what Lacan used to call "metonymy of being"—the elusive being that slides, slips away in the *défilé* of the signifiers, a being that exists only in the form of its lack (and which is the cause of desire). The notion of "para-being" (*par-être*), on the other hand, is what results from looking at the metonymy of being from another perspective, namely and precisely that of repetition.

We could say that in his late work, being as such is for Lacan essentially a (shifting) repetition of the impossible (of the "gap"), a repetition of that which is not. Being is not that which takes flight, eludes the grasp of the signifiers, but rather that which keeps repeating the "impossible" discontinuity at the heart of being. (We could perhaps say—referring back to Freud and his metaphors—that being is a circuitous repetition of the non-being at the very heart of being.)

This is what Lacan's so-called "para-ontology" (also sometimes referred to as "parontology") would be about: being is collateral (hence the expression "para-being") to its own impossibility, and not (as in Badiou) to the impossibility of the Event. That is to say: the impossibility that generates being (through displaced repetition) is the very same impossibility at stake in the Event (or "mobilized" by the Event). Or, in other terms, an Event is related to the very point of impossibility of being (its impossibility to be *qua being*). It is precisely because of this impossibility which it keeps repeating that being is a domain where things *can* happen; it has the potential for Events. And this, of course, is an important difference with regard to Badiou, for whom the interruption of being by an Event comes from an absolute "elsewhere."

What, then, would be a Lacanian definition of the Event? An Event occurs when something "stops not being written," as he puts it in *Seminar XX*. But how? Not by making the impossible possible, but by performing a *disjunction of the necessary and the impossible*. If the usual course (repetition) of being is in fact a conjunction of the impossible with the necessary (it "doesn't stop not being written"), an Event occurs when it stops not being written. What takes place with an Event is thus a disjunction that affirms being in its contingency (rather than in its neutrality). Lacan brings in this definition with respect to the event of love, or rather of the love encounter. The latter can have as a consequence that the sexual relation "stops not being written." Being no longer slips away, but coincides with the "you" that I love. "You are it!," "You are the being I've always been lacking!"

After making this point, however, Lacan concludes in a rather pessimistic way: beyond the (temporal) suspension of the non-relation, the love encounter has no means of sustaining this suspension in its contingency, hence it attempts to force its necessity. "All love, subsisting only on the basis of the 'stops not being written,' tends to make the negation shift to the 'doesn't stop being written,' doesn't stop, won't stop" (Lacan 1999, 145). This, then, is the move from contingency to necessity which "constitutes the destiny as well as the drama of love." It is my (im)modest claim—developed elsewhere—that "drama" is a significant word here, and that the comedy of love, or love as comedy, entails a different logic. But if it is indeed to work, the comedy of love is a much more demanding genre than the tragedy or drama of love. (And perhaps the same could be said for political events, namely, that a certain revolutionary "taste for drama" could well be something of a problem.)

Lacan's pessimistic conclusion in the quote above is of course not unrelated to the concept that Badiou introduces at this precise point—at the point of the question "What happens after the Event?"—namely, the concept of fidelity (not simply to our lover, but to the Event of our love encounter). Fidelity, and not just the Event itself, is what can eventually make a difference.

Lacan's reserve at this point could be attributed to his general "pessimism," or even to something rooted in his political views. But the actual emancipatory implications of the Lacanian theory are in no way confined by these political stances. This is why I am tempted to put forward the following suggestion.

What if we reintroduced here the notion of a "new signifier" as precisely that which could make it possible, in this case, to build something on the basis of a love encounter, without obscuring the contingency of (its) being?

A love (encounter) is not simply about everything falling into its rightful place. A love encounter is not simply about a contingent match between two different pathologies, about two individuals being lucky enough to encounter in each other what "works for them." Rather, love is what *makes it work*. Love *does* something to us. It makes, or allows for, the cause of our desire to condescend to, to coincide with, our lover. And the affect of this is *surprise*—only this surprise, and not simply our infatuation, is the sign of love proper. It is the sign of the subject, of the subjective figure of love. It says not simply: "You are it!," but rather: "How surprising that you are it!" Or, in a simpler formula of how love operates: *How surprising that you are you!*

In order to develop this in a more concrete way, it could be helpful to make a short digression and look at what Clément Rosset says about love in his book *Le Régime des passions*. Playing on the double meaning of the French word *régime*—system (of government) and diet)—Rosset develops his criticism of the notion of passion, which he sees as a morbid craving for an unreal (derealized, nonexistent or unattainable) object. Hence a passionate love, in contrast to "real love," always aims at objects that it cannot really have (and goes to great lengths to ensure just that); it is a passionate relationship with an unreal object. (Even if there is a concrete person behind it, as in Racine's *Phaedra*, this person is precisely irrelevant as a real person.) This is a love for an object the approach to which and enjoyment of which are infinitely deferred. According to Rosset, this amorous passion (which could be more appropriately called the passion of desire) is the opposite of love; it is like a war machine dedicated to paralyzing and forbidding. Hence

Phaedra "elects an object the enjoyment of which she forbids herself (I would even say that she elects him *so as not to enjoy him*), and then draws masochistic enjoyment from her very pain" (Rosset 2001, 16). For this is the other side of the "passion diet": it involves enjoyment not in the object of passion, but in the passionate dieting itself. (This is why Rosset rejects Saint-Simon's famous formula "Nothing great happens without passion," and replaces it with "Nothing mediocre happens without passion.") Rosset detects a similar passion structure (that is, an unappeasable craving for, and fascination with, an obscure and unreal object) in avarice and in the passion of collectors: the real objects of these passions don't really count. The miser never enjoys his treasure (or its value): "The miser is fascinated by the aura of unreality in which he makes his money swim, but not by the money itself" (ibid., 17). What thus defines passion, according to Rosset, is less a search for something than a quest for an object defined by two fundamental conditions: that it is obscure and indefinable, and at the same time outside any useful reach (that is, both out of reach and useless). And the more this is so, the greater the passion in its morbid self-perpetuating logic. This is precisely what makes Rosset link the logic of passion to what is the central topic of his philosophical work, namely, the theme of "the real and its double." To put it briefly: passion marks the hold that the fantasy of the double has over the perception of the real, the fascination with the absence provoked by the undesirable presence of a real which does not satisfy (or no longer satisfies) us, that is to say, the choice of the unreal to the detriment of the real. And one could add here that "revolutionary passion" actually often functions precisely in this way: as a passion for the "revolution" itself, rather than for patiently building a different world.

There is, however, something that Rosset skims over too quickly in his theory of passion, as well as in his theory of the double as simply an illusory redoubling of the real. In the opposition between the real object and the perverse enjoyment (in its deferral), real love is not simply on the side of the "real object" (as fully coinciding with itself). Moreover, one should insist that there is a certain degree of derealization or detachment involved in any real love, and this constitutes the very basis of the encounter and of the relationship with a concrete, "real" person. Paradoxically, this is something that Rosset himself very perspicaciously observes, without accepting the immediate consequences of this observation for his theory:

> Real love demands the reality of the loved person. Besides, the coincidence thanks to which a loved object is at the same time an existing object is, rather curiously, an inexhaustible subject of wonder for the lovers…: it is no longer "you are here" that counts, but the fact that "you *are* you." (Rosset 2001, 28)

This is precisely the formula we arrived at in our discussion above. Real love necessarily wonders at the coincidence of the loved (desired) object with an existing object. And this wondering is the affect of love proper.

In the terms of Rosset's arguments, this implies that there is something of the order of surprising coincidence that takes place also in real love, and hence presupposes a minimal difference or split—this split does not occur only with the illusory distortion (reduplication of the real, as he argues). And, as a matter of fact, the wonder here is no less comical than the one evoked in one of the jokes Freud quotes in his book on *Jokes and Their Relation to the Unconscious*: "He wondered how it is that cats have two holes cut in their skin precisely at the place where their eyes are" (Freud 1976, 97).

In order for the real lover to be nothing but the *coincidence* with herself, as Rosset himself maintains, there also needs to be a split, involving a minimal difference. It is precisely this minimal difference on account of which it makes sense to say, not *Je est un autre* (Rimbaud), but *tu est toi*, "you are you(rself)," which is the very condition (and form) of real love. It is not only that real love demands the reality of the loved person, it is also, and primarily, precisely about this *coincidence of the same* as the other side of its non-coincidence, made visible by the amorous encounter in the strong sense of the word. The split and the coincidence appear at the same time. Or: split appears as coincidence; they are, strictly speaking, one and the same.

In other words, we can agree with Rosset that "real love" is not the love that I would call sublime, the love in which we let ourselves be completely dazzled or "blinded" by an abstract dimension of the loved object, so that we no longer see, or can't bear to see, its concrete existence (and its always somewhat ridiculous, banal aspect). This kind of "sublime love" indeed necessitates and generates a radical inaccessibility of the other (which usually takes the form of eternal preliminaries, of an inaccessible object of choice, or the form of an intermittent relationship that enables us to reintroduce the distance appropriate to the inaccessible, and thereby to "resublimate" the object after each "use"). But neither is real love simply something that takes its object "such as it is," in the sense of homogeneity and (uninterrupted) continuity of its presence as real. It is only at the moment when we fall in love that a loved object "coincides" with an existing object, and this coincidence marks a break in the continuity of our (and our lover's) reality. This paradoxical—or, indeed, *comical*—coincidence is precisely what tears us (and our lover) from the continuity of our presence in reality, and it does so by (re)*installing us there*, as if for the first time.

An exchange in Marx Brothers' *A Night at the Opera* spells this out most directly. After sitting with another woman for quite a while, Groucho (Driftwood) comes to Mrs. Claypool's table (she has been waiting for him all this time), and the following dialogue ensues:

DRIFTWOOD (GROUCHO):   That woman? Do you know why I sat with her?

MRS. CLAYPOOL (MARGARET DUMONT):   No—

DRIFTWOOD: Because she reminded me of you.

MRS. CLAYPOOL: Really?

DRIFTWOOD: Of course! That's why I'm sitting here with you. Because you remind me of you. Your eyes, your throat, your lips, everything about you reminds me of you, except you. How do you account for that?

Comic subjects are best situated to produce genuine formulas of love. Indeed, come to think of it, is there any better answer to the impossible question: "Why do you love me?" than: "Because you remind me of yourself"?

Now, how do we relate all this to our discussion above? One way of understanding the notion of the "new signifier" would be precisely to see it as a signifier capable of naming, and hence sustaining, the minimal difference (contingency) on account of which my lover keeps reminding me of himself. In other words, to see it as precisely that which prevents the shift of negation that Lacan points out, the shift from "stops not being written" to "doesn't stop being written." What happens in this shift is that the impossibility disappears, and is simply replaced by necessity; but this disappearance of impossibility is not its solution, but its repression or foreclosure; hence the closing up of the very gap that made its "eventual" solution possible in the first place. In love, the impossible happens, and it is from there on that we must continue and work with what has happened, instead of assuming that from now on the impossible is (or should be) simply replaced by the possible and, indeed, necessary.

Since we have already ventured quite a long way onto the terrain of concrete examples, we can take a step further here and suggest a concrete example of a "new signifier" in the case of an amorous circumstance—with the obvious risk of the example striking us as rather banal with respect to our sublime expectations of what this *new* signifier might be. We shall take the risk. So what would be an example of a signifier capable of naming, and hence sustaining, the minimal difference (contingency) on account of which my lover keeps reminding me of himself? An example of a signifier that would prevent the gap of the "impossible" from simply disappearing from the scene (and returning in the Real)? Could we not say that a possible example of this would be the way in which a nickname sometimes functions in love relationships? And by this I certainly do not mean a "cute name" that one can pick from a list of such names, I mean a name that really names something in the relationship; a name that provides the signifier of the very (dis)junction of love object and existing object in a concrete love relationship. A name that works, works at generating and maintaining the *space* for construction at the precarious *point* of the Event. Such (nick)names (obviously, not all love nicknames work in this way, and there can also be something other than a nickname that does the job) usually have a comic sparkle to them, and this sparkle goes some distance in distracting the pathos of love as *destiny*.

Names, words—don't we have enough of those?

We started with sex (in its "impossibility"), and ended up with love in its evental dimension—which does not take us very far if it does not find its ally in some sort of signifying invention. This is where I want to stop. There are of course more general conclusions that one could develop from here, but I will restrict myself to just one brief remark. We often attribute the source of the evils of our time to the accelerating flow of ("just") words, specula- tion; to the lack of involvement with real things, real life, real experiences, and real emotions. Yet the problem is perhaps different: we have not lost the Real (which we never "had"), we are losing the *capacity of naming* that can have real effects, because it "hits" the right spot, the (dis)junction between the necessary and the Real (impossible). In all the profusion of words and more words, we lack the words that work. (Not what linguistics calls performatives, but words that can affect the economy of being because they come from the workings of this economy.) The turn to the Real (for example, to "real expe- rience") is part of the ideological warfare that diverts us from the only way in which we can touch something of the Real, which is precisely with the right word (and not simply with more words). The right word is not the same thing as a correct word, and it is certainly not about someone "being right" (or not); it is not simply the word that conveys, for example, the factual truth of what is going on. This is not about "efficiency" either. It is about words that name something about our reality for the first time, and hence make this something an object of the world, and of thought. There can be words and descriptions of reality prior to it, and there always are. But then there comes a word that gives us access to reality in a whole different way. It is not a cor- rect description of a reality; it introduces a new reality. When Marx wrote that "the history of all hitherto existing society is the history of class strug- gles," this is was not a description of social history that was more accurate than other descriptions. The concept of the class struggle is an example of a "new signifier," one that reveals a hitherto invisible dimension of social reality, and gives us tools to think it. It does so because it names the point where the impossibility of social justice gets disentangled from the necessity to repeat this impossibility.

FROM ADAM'S NAVEL TO DREAM'S NAVEL

After this excursion into the possible philosophical (and political) implications of the psychoanalytic concept of sexuality, let us conclude with what seems to be its most daring implication. Namely, that sexuality (as linked to the unconscious) is the point of a short circuit between ontology and epistemology: it is because of what is missing ("fallen out") from the signifying structuring of being that the unconscious, as a form of knowledge, relates to the impossibility of being involved in, and "transmitted" by, sexuality.

The theory that there exists a singular short circuit between ontological and epistemological dimensions is, of course, a very strong "philosophical" claim. Yet Freud himself suggested something of the sort in his account of the link between sexuality and knowledge: if sexuality is the drive of knowledge, it is not simply because we are curious about sex, or because we sublimate the lack of sex with a passion for knowledge. For the lack at stake is not a possible lack of sex, but a lack at the very heart of sex, or, more precisely, it concerns sex as the very structural incompleteness of being.

One of Freud's major theories concerns sexuality as the realm within which the quest (desire) for knowledge takes off. This Freudian genealogy of the passion for knowledge is in itself complex and intriguing, but its basic outline would be as follows:[1] There is no original drive for knowledge. It surfaces at points of existential difficulty: for example, when children feel threatened by the fact (or the possibility) of acquiring a sibling. Sexuality very soon becomes an obvious player in all questions about being (there) of oneself and of others. It enters the stage with the question of being ("How do we come to be?"), and it enters as negativity, as the unsatisfactory character of all possible positive answers. For while it is obviously involved in the becoming of being, sexuality nevertheless provides no point of attachment, no anchoring point, in the explication of being (as being). Moreover, for the inquisitive infant, sexuality is often bound up with stories and myths, embarrassment and avoidance, sometimes even with disgust and punishment.

Before we sigh that, well, this is again all about our petty little family stories and structures, it is crucial to acknowledge that the true question only begins at this point. It is not that these "family structures" can explain the Real of sexuality, but rather that something in the latter can explain, or point to, the gap that drives these structures. The embarrassment at and covering up of sexuality (by adults) should not be taken as self-explanatory, that is, as explained by the "traditional" cultural ban on sexuality, but rather the other way around. As I keep insisting, the cause of embarrassment in sexuality is not simply something which is there, on display in it, but on the contrary something that is not there, and is (or would be) of the order of knowledge. The fairytales with which we explain sexuality to children are there not so much in order to mask and distort the realistic explanation, but to mask the fact that there is no realistic explanation, and that even the most exhaustive scientific explanation lacks the signifier that would account for the sexual as sexual. What is at stake with this lack is thus not a missing piece of knowledge *about* the sexual (as a full entity in itself); what is at stake is that (drive) sexuality and knowledge are structured around a fundamental negativity, which unites them at the point of the unconscious. The unconscious is the concept of an inherent link between sexuality and knowledge in their very negativity.

The conclusion we can draw from all this would thus be the following: Whenever it comes to social, cultural, or religious covering up of sexuality, we can be sure that it never covers up simply what is there (for example, the sexual organs), but *also* (and perhaps primarily) something which is not there; it also covers up some fundamental ambiguity which is, from the outset, of a *metaphysical order*. In other words: the more we try to think the sexual as sexual (that is, the more we try to think it only for "what it is," without censorship and embellishments), the quicker we find ourselves in the element of pure and profound metaphysics. This is why there is no "*neutral*" way to speak about sex—even if we pretend not to hide anything, and speak only of facts, something else seems to get added, or to disappear....

A vivid and direct illustration of this can be found in the form of a problem that early artists faced when they painted Adam and Eve, a problem that relates these questions to our earlier discussion of realism. The problem the artists faced was the following: Should they portray the first couple with or without navels? Adam was molded from spit and clay, Eve from Adam's rib. They were not born of women, so how could they have navels? Yet they looked strange without them: they were the first humans, and they should look like (other) humans. But if as humans they were created in God's image, God also has to have a navel, which generates new conceptual difficulties.... (This illustrates the dilemma that Gosse was facing when he was trying to reconcile the geological age of fossils with God's creation according to Genesis: his answer was that when God created Adam, he also created the navel, that is to say, his "ancestry." ...) So the problem the artists faced was quite real; and they often dodged the question by extending fig leaves so that they covered not only the sexual organs, but the lower belly as well.

Is not this extending of the fig leaves to hide more than just sexual organs a perfect illustration of the argument I am making here? Namely, that by covering up "the sexual," one always also—and perhaps primarily?—covers up something else, something that is not there and which tends to raise some deeply metaphysical issues and ambiguities. And it should come as no surprise that it is precisely this additional point that is the principal locus of myths and fantasies about procreation and about (our) origins. Different theological theories surrounding the issue of Adam's navel—for example, the "Pre-Umbilist," "Mid-Umbilist," and "Post-Umbilist" theories—constitute fascinating reading.

The extended fig leaf covers not simply the sexual, but the navel as the elected figure of the scar left by the lapse of being—the lapse of being involved in sexuation (and sexual reproduction). If sexuality seems to exist only on the ontic level, and to have no proper ontological dignity, the reason is not that it corresponds to nothing on the ontological level, but rather that it corresponds to a gap inside this ontological level.

And, speaking of navels, it is of course no coincidence that we find in Freud (in *The Interpretation of Dreams*) the famous, as well as curious, expression: *der Nabel des Traums*, "the dream's navel," related not to what we can know, but to the hole in the very net of knowledge that can be laid out in the analytic interpretation.

> There is often a passage in even the most thoroughly interpreted dream
> which has to be left obscure; this is because we become aware during the
> work of interpretation that at that point there is a tangle of dream-thoughts
> which cannot be unraveled and which moreover adds nothing to our
> knowledge of the content of the dream. This is the dream's navel, the spot
> where it reaches down into the unknown. (Freud 1988, 671)

I would suggest that we should read the term "unknown" not as referring to something "unknown to us," but in a stronger sense of the gap in knowledge coinciding with the gap in being. We do not know, because there is nothing to know. Yet this "nothing" is inherent to being, and constitutes its irreducible crack; it registers as a peculiar ("negative") epistemological score, it registers as a peculiar form of knowledge: the unconscious.

CHAPTER 1

1. See Shalev and Yerushalmi 2009.

2. For more on these questions, see Zupančič 2008, 20–23.

3. See, for example, Laplanche 1999, 258.

4. In *De nuptiis et concupiscentia* (On Marriage and Concupiscence), chapter 7.

5. See, for example, Alacoque 1995.

6. For a really impressive collection of these images, it suffices to search the Internet for Saint Agatha (and Saint Lucy)—images.

7. The "doctrine speaks of the incarnation of God in a body, and assumes that the passion suffered in that person constituted another person's *jouissance*" (Lacan 1999, 113).

8. They sometimes do very "strange" things as part of sexual (mating) rituals, but they do not seem to find anything "strange" about it, it does not seem to bother them in the least.

9. Žižek made this point by suggesting that "there is no sexual relation" should be changed to "there is sexual non-relation" (Žižek 2012, 796).

CHAPTER 2

1. For an exhaustive commentary on these questions, see Dolar 2007, 14–38.

2. This is why the only way to approach sex, to talk about it, is to take it as a logical problem (or an onto-logical problem). In this way we perhaps stand a chance of getting at some kind of real. On the other hand, if we approach it as a problem of the body and its sensations, we are bound to end up in the imaginary (or in metaphysics).

3. See also Slavoj Žižek's powerful discussion of the non-relation in Žižek 2012, 794–802.

4. To some extent, the more recent idea of the "post-human" also belongs to this tradition of conceiving emancipation as essentially emancipation from the "human."

5. See Lacan 1987, 194–196.

6. The formulation "concrete constitutive negativity" requires further explanation. In general theoretical terms, we should say of this configuration: it is not that there is one fundamental non-relation and a multiplicity of different relations, determined by the former in a negative way. It is, rather, that every relationship also posits the concrete point of the impossible that determines it. It determines what will be determining it. In this sense we could say that all social relations are concretizations of the non-relation as universal determination of the discursive, which does not exist anywhere outside these concrete (non-)relations. This also means that the non-relation is not the ultimate (ontological) foundation of the discursive, but its surface—it exists and manifests itself only through it. To put it differently: it is not that there is (and remains) a fundamental non-relation which will never be (re)solved by any concrete relation. Rather: every concrete relation *de facto* resolves the non-relation, but it can resolve it only by positing ("inventing"), together with itself, its own negativity, its own negative condition/impossibility. The non-relation is not something that "insists" and "remains," but something that is repeated—something that "does not stop not being written" (to use Lacan's expression). It is not something that resists all writing, and that no writing can actually write—it is inherent to writing, and repeats itself with it.

CHAPTER 3

1. For more on this, see Lacan 1987, 151.

2. I will not discuss here whether the Kantian gesture simply closed the door behind ontology, or laid the ground for a new and quite different kind of ontology.

3. See, for example, Butler 1990.

4. "It is essential to understand clearly that the concepts 'masculine' and 'feminine,' whose meaning seems so unambiguous to ordinary people, are among the most confused that occur in science."

5. See Zupančič 2008, 59–60.

6. This, of course, is also one of the key points of Žižek's reading of both. See, for example, Žižek 2012.

7. For more on this, see Dolar 2010.

8. Copjec 1994, Žižek 2012, Le Gaufey 2006, Chiesa 2016—to mention just a few.

9. Lacan insists that the Woman is one of the names of the Father.

10. This, of course, is also what is at stake in fetishism.

11. As Mladen Dolar summed this up most succinctly: "the sexual difference poses the problem of the two precisely because it cannot be reduced to the binary opposition or accounted for in terms of the binary numerical two. It is not a signifying difference, such that it defines the elements of structure. It is not to be described in terms of opposing features, or as a relation of given entities preexisting the difference. . . . The two that we are after is not the binary two of equal or different ones, but the two of the one and the Other. One could say: bodies can be counted, sexes cannot.

Sex presents a limit to the count of bodies, it cuts them from inside rather than grouping them together under common headings" (Dolar 2010, 88).

12. This difference between two kinds of differences, a relational one and a non-relational one, is what Lacan develops in detail, and in relation to set theory, in his late seminars, and I will discuss it in chapter 4 below.

13. Mladen Dolar developed this in some detail in Dolar 2010.

14. Starting with her magnum opus *L'effet sophistique* (Paris: Gallimard, 1995).

15. Badiou recounts this anecdote in "The Scene of Two" (see Badiou 2003, 43).

16. See Badiou and Cassin 2010, 109.

17. Lacan keeps repeating that he is a "realist" rather than a nominalist or an idealist.

18. In a lecture delivered in Ljubljana in February 2016.

19. Mladen Dolar, "Two Shades of Gray," lecture delivered at the Beckett Conference, Freie Universität Berlin, February 1, 2016. Emphasis added.

CHAPTER 4

1. This is why Slavoj Žižek is right to point out that the cost of this kind of materialism might well be a re-spiritualization of matter (see Žižek 2010, 303), as is the case of Jane Bennett's notion of "vibrant matter." Needless to say, however, my cursory reference to Malabou here fails to do justice to her argument in its entirety, as well as to some very valuable points that she makes in presenting it.

2. See Chiesa 2010, 159–177.

3. "If I am anything, it is clear that I'm not a nominalist. I mean that my starting point is not that the name is something that one sticks, like this, on the real. And one must choose. If we are nominalists, we must completely renounce dialectical materialism, so that, in short, the nominalist tradition, which is strictly speaking the only danger of idealism that can occur in a discourse like mine, is quite obviously ruled out. This is not about being realist in the sense one was realist in the Middle Ages, that is in the sense of the realism of the universals; what is at stake is to mark off the fact that our discourse, our scientific discourse, finds the real only in that it depends on the function of the semblance" (Lacan 2006b, 28).

4. His argument in this respect is that correlationist philosophy, precisely since it claims that we can know nothing about things in themselves, forces us to admit that even the most irrational obscurantist nonsense talked about things in themselves is at least possible.

5. Zupančič 2008.

6. And we actually find this idea in Nietzsche, when he says: "Let us beware of saying that death is opposed to life. The living is merely a type of what is dead, and a very rare type" (Nietzsche 1974, 168). We find a similar idea (with an additional twist) in Freud, and we shall return to it in the Conclusion.

7. See Chiesa 2016.

8. I was led to make this connection between the Freudian death drive and fatigue when I was invited to speak at the Pembroke Research Seminar (Brown University) on "Fatigue," led by Joan Copjec, in 2015–2016.

9. "The tension which then arose in what had hitherto been inanimate substance endeavored to cancel itself out. In this way the first instinct came into being: the instinct to return to the inanimate state."

10. Freud 2001b, 53. Jung adopted the Freudian notion of the libido and, with an apparently small modification, gave it an entirely different meaning. With Jung, the libido becomes a psychic expression of a "vital energy," the origin of which is not solely sexual. In this perspective, libido is a general name for psychic energy, which is sexual only in certain segments. Freud immediately saw how following this Jungian move would entail sacrificing "all that we have gained hitherto from psychoanalytic observation" (Freud 1977a, 140).

11. Germ cells are capable of an independent existence. "Under favorable conditions, they begin to develop—that is, to repeat the performance to which they owe their existence; and in the end once again one portion of their substance pursues its development to a finish, while another portion harks back once again as a fresh residual germ to the beginning of the process of development" (Freud 2001b, 40).

12. In this precise sense, Lacan will identify instincts with a "knowledge in the Real" as precisely "knowledge" of these paths.

13. In "The Ego and the Id," Freud famously defined the superego as "pure culture of the death-instinct."

14. In the context of the Freudian theory of the sexual seduction of children (and the possible "trauma" related to it), Jean Laplanche has convincingly argued that this kind of alternative is wrong, or too simple. Freud first posited the sexual seduction of children by adults as real, that is to say, as a factual/empirical event in the child's history, which is then repressed and can become the ground or *cause* of different symptoms and neurotic disturbances. Later, he abandoned this theory in favor of the theory of the fantasy of seduction: generally speaking, seduction is not an event that takes place in empirical reality, but a fantasy constructed later, in the period of our sexual awareness, and it exists only in the psychic reality of the subject. Approached with the tool of the distinction between material reality and psychic reality (fantasy), the question of sexual seduction leads either to the claim that everything is material seduction (for how exactly are we to isolate and define the latter: does touching a baby's lips, for example, or its bottom, qualify as seduction?) or to the conclusion that seduction is entirely fantasmatic, mediated by the psychic reality of the one who "feels seduced." Laplanche's answer to this conflict between raw materialism and psychological idealism is profoundly materialistic in the sense that he recognizes a properly *material* cause, yet a cause that cannot be reduced to (or deduced from) what has empirically happened in the interaction between the child and the adult. In other words, according to Laplanche, the true trigger of the subsequent constitution of the unconscious lies neither in raw material reality nor in the ideal reality of fantasy, but is the very materiality of a third reality, which is transversal to the other two and

which Laplanche calls the material reality of the enigmatic message. For more on this, see Laplanche 1999.

15. Again, we find a similar move in Laplanche's theory according to which "psychic reality" is not created by us, but is essentially *invasive*; it comes, it invades us from the outside, where it is already constituted (as the unconscious of others). See Laplanche 1999.

16. Deleuze uses the term "death instinct," following the then current French translation of the Freudian *Todestrieb*.

17. Hence Deleuze writes, for example, that even when we are dealing with something that appears to be repetition of the same (such as, for instance, the rituals in obsessional neurosis), we have to recognize in the element that is being repeated— that is, in the repetition of the same—the mask of a deeper repetition (Deleuze 1994, 17).

18. And Deleuze actually attributes this reversal to Freud, and to his hypothesis of "primal repression."

19. "For when Freud shows beyond repression 'properly speaking,' which bears upon *representations*—the necessity of supposing a primary repression which concerns first and foremost pure *presentations*, or the manner in which the drives are necessarily lived, we believe that he comes closest to a positive internal principle of repetition. This later appears to him determinable in the form of the death instinct, and it is this which, far from being explained by it, must explain the blockage of representation in repression properly speaking" (Deleuze 1994, 18).

20. Quoted in Deleuze 1990, 331.

21. Ibid., 321; emphasis added.

22. Ibid., 322.

23. Ibid., 325.

24. Discussing his "myth" of the lamella (related to the death drive), Lacan writes: "It is the libido, *qua* pure life instinct, that is to say immortal life, or irrepressible life, life that has need of no organ, simplified, indestructible life. It is precisely what is subtracted from the living being by virtue of the fact that it is subject to the cycle of sexed reproduction. And it is of this that all the forms of the *objet a* that can be enumerated are the representatives, the equivalents. The *objets a* are merely its representatives, its figures. The breast—as equivocal, as an element characteristic of the mammiferous organization, the placenta for example—certainly represents that part of himself that the individual loses at birth, and which may serve to symbolize the most profound lost object. I could make the same kind of reference for all the other objects" (Lacan 1987, 198).

25. In this sense, what Foucault says about the "repressive hypothesis" is quite correct (and he is actually repeating Lacan's point here): In modern societies, sexuality has been *anything but* repressed; we have been witnessing—with respect to sexuality—a gigantic "incitement to discourse," an "implantation of perversity," a gesture of bringing sexuality into focus and under the spotlight, seeing it everywhere, making,

even forcing it, to speak all the time. What is lacking from Foucault's account is, quite simply, the notion of the unconscious and of "repression" in the Freudian sense (*Verdrängung*), which is not mentioned one single time in the entire first volume of the *History of Sexuality*. From a Lacanian point of view, the discursive proliferation of sexuality (and its exploitation) is made possible only by its structural relation to the unconscious as the "founding negativity" of sexuality itself. For a more detailed discussion of this, see Zupančič 2016.

26. Although one should stress that very often they do not come even close to the complexity of Deleuzian philosophy.

27. Quoted in Žižek 2012, 32. I will not repeat Žižek's argument, which I cannot but agree with, but will use this quote for my own purposes.

28. This, for example, is the basic move we find in Levi Bryant's otherwise very complex work *The Democracy of Objects* (Bryant 2011).

29. In this sense, Hegel may well be the philosophical materialist *par excellence*. As Mladen Dolar has pointed out: in direct opposition to a long (Aristotelian) tradition, aligning truth with the principle of non-contradiction, Hegel took a very different step with the first of his "habilitation theses" (which served as the basis of his PhD defense in August 1801) when he said: "Contradictio est regula veri, non contradictio falsi"—Contradiction is the rule of truth, non-contradiction of the false (Dolar 1990, 20).

30. Slavoj Žižek has developed this point on several occasions.

31. As Lacan puts it in a lecture from his Seminar *Les non-dupes errent* (May 21, 1974).

32. This, for example, is what Gabriel Tupinambá suggests in an article where he picks up this topic. See Tupinambá 2015.

33. If we have a multiple of, say, five elements, the possible combination of these elements—that is to say, the number of the "parts"—exceeds by far the number of elements (more precisely, this number amounts to 2 to the power of 5).

CONCLUSION

1. See, for example, Freud 1977b.

BIBLIOGRAPHY

Alacoque, Margaret Mary. 1995. *The Autobiography of Saint Margaret Mary*. Charlotte: TAN Books.

Althusser, Louis. 1993. "Sur Marx et Freud." In *Écrits sur la psychanalyse*. Paris: STOCK/IMEC.

Aristotle. 1999. *The Metaphysics*. Harmondsworth, UK: Penguin.

Badiou, Alain. 1999. *Manifesto for Philosophy*. Albany: SUNY Press.

Badiou, Alain. 2003. "The Scene of Two." *Lacanian Ink* 21.</

Badiou, Alain. 2005. *Being and Event*. London: Continuum.

Badiou, Alain. 2009. *Logics of the Worlds*. London: Continuum.

Badiou, Alain, and Barbara Cassin. 2010. *Il n'y a pas de rapport sexuel*. Paris: Fayard.

Brassier, Ray. 2007. *Nihil Unbound*. New York: Palgrave Macmillan.

Bryant, Levi R. 2011. *The Democracy of Objects*. Ann Arbor: Open Humanities Press.

Butler, Judith. 1990. *Gender Trouble: Feminism and the Subversion of Identity*. London: Routledge.

Cassin, Barbara. 1995. *L'effet sophistique*. Paris: Gallimard.

Chiesa, Lorenzo. 2010. "Hyperstructuralism's Necessity of Contingency." In *S: Journal of the Jan van Eyck Circle for Lacanian Ideology Critique* 3.

Chiesa, Lorenzo. 2016. *The Not-Two: Logic and God in Lacan*. Cambridge, MA: MIT Press.

Copjec, Joan. 1994. *Read My Desire: Lacan against the Historicists*. Cambridge, MA: MIT Press.

Copjec, Joan. 2012. "The Sexual Compact." *Angelaki* 17 (2).

Deleuze, Gilles. 1990. *The Logic of Sense*. London: Athlone Press.

Deleuze, Gilles. 1994. *Difference and Repetition.* New York: Columbia University Press.

Dolar, Mladen. 1990. *Fenomenologija duha I.* Ljubljana: Društvo za teoretsko psihoanalizo.

Dolar, Mladen. 2006. *A Voice and Nothing More.* Cambridge, MA: MIT. Press.

Dolar, Mladen. 2007. "Freud und das Politische." *Texte. Psychoanalyse, Ästhetik, Kulturkritik* (Vienna), 2007, no. 4.

Dolar, Mladen. 2010. "One Splits into Two." *Die Figur der Zwei/The Figure of Two. Das Magazin des Instituts für Theorie,* no. 14/15.

Freud, Sigmund. 1976. *Jokes and Their Relation to the Unconscious.* Pelican Freud Library 6. Harmondsworth, UK: Penguin.

Freud, Sigmund. 1977a. Three Essays on the Theory of Sexuality. In *On Sexuality.* Pelican Freud Library 7. Harmondsworth, UK: Penguin.

Freud, Sigmund. 1977b. On the Sexual Theories of Children. In *On Sexuality.* Pelican Freud Library 7. Harmondsworth, UK: Penguin.

Freud, Sigmund. 1988. *The Interpretation of Dreams.* Harmondsworth, UK: Penguin.

Freud, Sigmund. 2001a. "Repression." In *The Standard Edition of the Complete Psychological Works of Sigmund Freud.* Vol. 14. London: Vintage Books.

Freud, Sigmund. 2001b. Beyond the Pleasure Principle. In *The Standard Edition of the Complete Psychological Works of Sigmund Freud.* vol. 18. London: Vintage Books.

Freud, Sigmund. 2001c. 'Wild' Psycho-Analysis. In *The Standard Edition of the Complete Psychological Works of Sigmund Freud.* vol. 11. London: Vintage Books.

Gould, Stephen Jay. 1985. "Adam's Navel." In *The Flamingo's Smile: Reflections in Natural History.* Harmondsworth, UK: Penguin.

Hardin, Garrett. 1982. *Naked Emperors: Essays of a Taboo-Stalker.* Los Altos, CA: William Kaufmann.

Hegel, G. W. F. 1977. *Phenomenology of Spirit.* Trans. A. V. Miller. Oxford: Oxford University Press.

Lacan, Jacques. 1973. "L'étourdit." *Scilicet* 4.

Lacan, Jacques. 1976. "Conférences et entretiens dans des universités nord-américaines." *Scilicet* 6–7.

Lacan, Jacques. 1987. *The Four Fundamental Concepts of Psychoanalysis.* Harmondsworth, UK: Penguin.

Lacan, Jacques. 1988. *The Seminar of Jacques Lacan. Book II: The Ego in Freud's Theory and in the Technique of Psychoanalysis.* New York: W. W. Norton.

Lacan, Jacques. 1990. *Television: A Challenge to the Psychoanalytic Establishment.* New York: W. W. Norton.

Lacan, Jacques. 1999. *Encore. The Seminar of Jacques Lacan, Book XX.* New York: W. W. Norton.

Lacan, Jacques. 2006a. *Le Séminaire, livre XVI. D'un autre à l'Autre.* Paris: Seuil.

Lacan, Jacques. 2006b. *Le Séminaire, livre XVIII. D'un discours qui ne serait pas du semblant.* Paris: Seuil.

Lacan, Jacques. 2006c. *Écrits.* New York: W. W. Norton.

Lacan, Jacques. 2007. *The Other Side of Psychoanalysis.* New York: W. W. Norton.

Lacan, Jacques. 2011. *Le Séminaire, livre XIX.... ou pire.* Paris: Seuil.

Laplanche, Jean. 1999. "La psychoanalyse comme anti-herméneutique." In *Entre séduction et inspiration.* Paris: Presses Universitaires de France.

Laplanche, Jean. 2002. "Sexuality and Attachment in Metapsychology." In *Infantile Sexuality and Attachment,* ed. Daniel Widlöcher. New York: Other Press.

Le Gaufey, Guy. 2006. *Le Pastout de Lacan: Consistence logique, conséquences cliniques.* Paris: EPEL.

Malabou, Catherine. 2007. *Les nouveaux blessés.* Paris: Bayard.

Marx, Karl. 1990. *Capital.* Vol. 1. Harmondsworth, UK: Penguin.

Meillassoux, Quentin. 2008. *After Finitude.* London: Continuum.

Miller, Jacques-Alain. 1996. "On Perversion." In *Reading Seminars I and II,* ed. Bruce Fink et al. Albany: State University of New York Press.

Miller, Jacques-Alain. 2000. "Paradigms of Jouissance." *Lacanian Ink* 17.

Milner, Jean-Claude. 2008. *Le Périple structural.* Lagrasse: Verdier.

Nietzsche, Friedrich. 1974. *The Gay Science.* Trans. Walter Kaufmann. New York: Vintage Books.

Platonov, Andrei. 2013. "The Anti-Sexus." *Cabinet Magazine,* no. 51.

Riviere, Joan. 1929. "Womanliness as Masquerade." *International Journal of Psychoanalysis* 10.

Rosset, Clément. 2001. *Le Régime des passions.* Paris: Minuit.

Schuster, Aaron. 2013. "Sex and Anti-Sex." *Cabinet Magazine,* no. 51.

Schuster, Aaron. 2016. *The Trouble with Pleasure: Deleuze and Psychoanalysis.* Cambridge, MA: MIT Press.

Shalev, Ofra, and Hanoch Yerushalmi. 2009. "Status of Sexuality in Contemporary Psychoanalytic Psychotherapy as Reported by Therapists." *Psychoanalytic Psychology* 26.

Smith, Adam. 2005. *An Inquiry into the Nature and Causes of the Wealth of Nations.* Mechanicsville, VA: Electric Book Co.

Tupinambá, Gabriel. 2015. "Vers un Signifiant Nouveau: Our Task after Lacan." In *Repeating Žižek*, ed. Agon Hamza. Durham: Duke University Press.

Zamanian, Kaveh. 2011. "Attachment Theory as Defense: What Happened to Infantile Sexuality?" *Psychoanalytic Psychology* 28 (1).

Žižek, Slavoj. 1989. *The Sublime Object of Ideology.* London: Verso.

Žižek, Slavoj. 1999. *The Ticklish Subject.* London: Verso.

Žižek, Slavoj. 2004. *Organs without Bodies.* London: Routledge.

Žižek, Slavoj. 2008. *In Defense of Lost Causes.* London: Verso.

Žižek, Slavoj. 2010. *Living in the End of Times.* London: Verso.

Žižek, Slavoj. 2012. *Less than Nothing.* London: Verso.

Zupančič, Alenka. 2008. *Why Psychoanalysis: Three Interventions.* Uppsala: NSU Press.

Zupančič, Alenka. 2016. "Biopolitics, Sexuality and the Unconscious." *Paragraph* 29 (1).